~~~~~~~~~~~~~~~~~~~~

I Loved,
I Lost,
I Made Spaghetti

A Memoir

~~~~~~~~~~~~~~~~~~~~

Giulia Melucci

GRAND CENTRAL
PUBLISHING

LARGE PRINT

Grand Central Publishing
Hachette Book Group
237 Park Avenue
New York, NY 10017

Visit our Web site at www.HachetteBookGroup.com

Printed in the United States of America

First Edition: April 2009
10 9 8 7 6 5 4 3 2 1

Grand Central Publishing is a division of
Hachette Book Group, Inc.
The Grand Central Publishing name and logo is a trademark
of Hachette Book Group, Inc.

Library of Congress Cataloging-in-Publication Data

Melucci, Giulia.
    I loved, I lost, I made spaghetti / Giulia Melucci. — 1st ed.
        p. cm.
    Summary: "A Brooklyn-based publicist's account of her
relationships gone awry, and the food that sustained her
through it all." —Provided by the publisher.
    ISBN 978-0-446-53442-0 (regular ed.)
    ISBN 978-0-446-55232-5 (large print ed.)
    1. Food.   2. Cookery, Italian.   3. Man-woman
relationships. 4. Melucci, Giulia.   I. Title.
    TX357.M488   2009
    641.5945—dc22   2008040732

The Large Print edition published in accord with the
standards of the N.A.V.H

*For my mother, who taught me how to cook
and how to love*

AUTHOR'S NOTE: Most of the names and some of the identifying details have been changed to protect the innocent and less so.

Contents

I Loved,
I Lost, I Made Spaghetti

~~~~~~~

Antipasto

~~~~~~~

Whenever I start dating someone new, I just can't hold back. No matter how often my girlfriends warn me, "Take it slow, let him win you over, don't give it away so quickly," I just can't resist—I have to cook for him.

For me, a new boyfriend is a tantalizing opportunity to show off the thing I'm most confident about: my cooking. I assess the gastronomic inclinations of the man in question at first sight, and my guesses are usually right. I've made every kind of food from simple pastas to slow-cooking stews and moist, beautifully seasoned roasts accompanied by perfectly browned potatoes and bright, crisp vegetables. I've made chocolate cakes, cheesecakes, and cakes filled with seasonal fruits. And I've dated every sort of man: artist, lawyer, banker, and writer, kind and unkind, ready to commit and as amenable to commitment as I am to eating at the Olive Garden.

In each of my relationships, I have honed my skills and developed my own style and assurance in the kitchen. The men who have passed through my life have all been culinary inspirations, and if I haven't figured out anything about love, at the very least I have learned how to cook with the greatest simplicity, delivering the maximum flavor, because when you're in love you want time for other things besides food. But good food is the best complement I can think of to the many pleasures love offers. It can also be the greatest comfort for the pain it can sometimes cause. I am not talking about obvious remedies, like pints of ice cream! That has never been my style. No,

the best balm for a broken heart is nour-
ishing food you make in your kitchen (or
better yet, food cooked for you by a dear
friend; I am fortunate to have many who
are great cooks). Food that tells your
heart and mind that you are taking care
of yourself, at least for now, until the next
man comes along, as he always does, and
you're happily cooking for two again.

Kit Fraser
Would Prefer
a Drink

I got a late start on the whole dating
thing.

Kit Fraser was my first real boyfriend. He entered my life in January
1990, the day after I moved into my first
New York apartment: an East Village sublet I shared with Jennifer Warren, a close
friend from college. For the first eighteen
months after graduation, I lived with my
mother in the house where I grew up in
Brooklyn. This was not exactly my ideal
postcollege habitat; the transition to a
place of my own had been delayed by my
father's death, which occurred simultaneously with the end of school. I was loath

to leave my mother alone in that big gray stucco house, but I was also fed up with my two brothers using the basement for band practice while their girlfriends sat in the kitchen helping themselves to the provisions as if they owned the place. It was loud and it was uncomfortable. I had to get out.

That Monday morning, Lucy, my boss at *Spy* magazine, the legendary satirical monthly where I was employed as a picture researcher, said to me: "Now that you have a new apartment, you'll probably get a new boyfriend." What new boyfriend? I thought. There had never been an old one. Well, at least not for any significant amount of time.

Up until then, the only man I could honestly have called a boyfriend was Steve Sullivan, a local boy four years my senior whom I dated for about four weeks around the time of my sixteenth birthday. I remember this because Steve took me on a real grown-up date to a restaurant to celebrate and gave me a bracelet made of jade beads for a present. He wore a coat and tie—and I, a dress from Bergdorf Goodman. My mother played it free and easy with her stash of department-store-specific charge cards in those days, sending me into "the city," as we called it, for shopping and haircuts at Bergdorf's, the quintessence of elegance, on a regular basis. I would also have on my person a note in her scrawl explaining that I had permission to use the card, just in case anyone questioned me (they never did).

I considered myself a punk rocker back then, and the dress was a Bergdorf Goodman take on punk: The top half of it was made of aqua T-shirt fabric cut off sloppily at the neck and sleeves, while the bottom was white cotton, gathered and painted by hand. I thought it was just the right level of sophistication for Steve, who was in college but lived at home and liked to hang out with his sister Lizzie's friends, among whose number I counted myself, if only marginally.

I grew up in Bay Ridge, a neighborhood that—tragically—is best known for being the setting of *Saturday Night Fever,* a movie that did about as much for Italian-Americans as the Gotti family. Although the film may have contained some truths, we liked to believe they were Bensonhurst's truths. The neighborhood I knew had Irish families as well as Italian. My friends had real problems: divorced parents, parents who were alcoholics, or both; siblings who were addicted to drugs. But they didn't turn to the disco floor to get a sense of mastery over their troubles; they made jokes. Any time there was a homeless-looking man walking down the street, my best friend in high school, Denise O'Dea, would wail pathetically: "Daddyyyyyyyyy! Daddy, come hooooooooooome!" I still think this is funny.

Denise and I would go to the Sullivans' every day after school. There Lizzie held court over a throng of her former classmates from Our Lady of Angels, a parish school that stood directly across the street from her house. I was somewhat in awe of the girls who went there, as they played basketball and attended classes with boys. My primary education at Visitation Academy, an all-girls school run by cloistered nuns situated behind big stone walls that wrapped around an entire city block, was a bit more precious and left me with no inclination whatsoever to dribble.

Still, it was a fun group to hang out with, so hang out we did. Steve got a kick out of us while he himself maintained an air of superiority: He went to Fordham University and attended the ballet; he would argue with my father about the war in the Falklands. After he railed against British "self-determination" (being Irish, he was against it), we would go make out on a piano bench—the only seat that accommodated two in the enclosed front porch of my family's house. While listening to Billy Joel's "She's Got a Way" on the record player in my basement, I thought to myself, This must be

exactly what he feels about me. I, however, wasn't so sure about him. I got a
little queasy thinking about him when
he wasn't around, though when I was
with him it was fun. I liked kissing him,
but I had no interest in going any further.
"You can touch me if you want to," he
cooed once during a make-out session.
Why ever would I want to do a thing like
that? I thought.

One evening on the piano bench, Steve
declared that he was going to give it a go
with the woman he had always wanted,
Bernadette Corrigan. She was a big girl,
a basketball player; her father owned a
tugboat company, and their family had
money. My father was a golfing buddy of
Bernadette's father and helped him get
into the country club. (And this was the
thanks we got!) Two months later, Bernadette was on the Sullivan stoop showing off the gifts Steve got her for her
birthday—those Russian dolls that open
up to reveal smaller and smaller dolls
inside, with the last doll containing a

Claddagh ring (the Irish wedding band, though they weren't engaged). I came up with imaginative reasons why this scene wasn't an excruciatingly painful one for me to watch.

The year before I got together with Kit, I had been seeing a psychologist—a strict Freudian who resembled Cher—to get to the bottom of why, at twenty-three, I had never had a boyfriend for any significant amount of time and had not yet had sex. I was haunted by my lack of experience and convinced I would die a virgin. I felt alienated from my friends (late starters all, but I was the latest), who had been let in on some cosmic secret that remained a mystery to me. The odds were against me for more reasons than just my neuroses: I had gone to all-girls schools until college, and then to Sarah Lawrence, where the female-to-male ratio was four to one—really more like eight to one, considering that the majority of the "ones" were gay. Every boy who wanted a girlfriend at Sarah Lawrence already had one or even two. It was survival of the fittest, and I was neither physically (I was a little plump) nor mentally (I was terrified) fit enough to compete with the willowy bohemian heiresses who surrounded me.

Without particularly wanting to, I remained the good Catholic girl. The only reputation I ever had was for being funny. The cruel truth that men might prefer to get their yuks in one place and their ya-yas in another was brought home to me in my thirteenth summer when I discovered that Tony Sirianni, my constant companion at the country club pool, was spending his nights on the golf course making out with Connie Cambria. Granted, Connie looked a lot better in a bathing suit than I did. At college, I spent countless late nights talking to boys I had crushes on, but the activities never went past conversation or, that great tease, listening to music. The sheets and my virtue always remained pristine when we parted in the wee hours. I didn't know if I was doing something wrong, giving off some bad vibe, or misreading whatever signal they were throwing. I did know it had me totally flummoxed, a conclusion I could have drawn without a psychologist's corroboration.

That was behind me now. A new decade was beginning; my boss and I decided to call it "the decade of love." Her prediction concerning the change in my romantic status proved strangely prescient. That very afternoon, a hand-delivered letter arrived from Kit Fraser. I had met Kit three years earlier when he showed up unexpectedly at my family's house one summer evening with Michael Petriano, the brother of my oldest friend, Larisa. She and her family had moved to New Jersey after first grade, but despite the distance, our friendship continued with regular weekend visits in New Jersey or Brooklyn right through high school. I enjoyed getting to experience the lures of suburbia—sundaes from Friendly's and public school (with boys and no uniforms), to which I would accompany

Larisa when I took a day off to see her. Larisa still lives in New Jersey, and we remain friends thirty-five years later.

Michael was my first crush. When I was ten I would join him on his paper routes, getting up at five in the morning to have some time alone together, riding Larisa's borrowed bicycle around the neighborhood. Michael was brilliant and incredibly funny, and for this he suffered. He had a nervous breakdown the summer after he graduated high school; the week he appeared on my doorstep with Kit, he had chosen to go off his meds, and in my childhood bedroom he ranted about the bomb he was going to create to eradicate evil from the earth, which would be controlled by a specially selected group of clerics and rabbis. Then he went to take a shower.

While Michael was in the bathroom and my mother went about the house hiding sharp objects, Kit watched me unpack my books from the school year that had just ended. I talked to him about my current intellectual obsession, Dante, and played him an Aztec Camera record. According to Kit (I don't remember this), I strung a bunch of tiny seed beads and tied them around his ankle. The evening stayed in Kit's mind not just because of our friend's odd behavior, but because of me. The bracelet stayed on his ankle until it fell apart, and when it did, he kept the pieces.

Two years later, while waiting for the elevator up to the *Spy* offices after lunch, I noticed a cute preppy guy wearing wire-rimmed glasses and an L.L.Bean hunting jacket waiting there, too. I wondered where he was going and became even more curious when he got out on my floor. He walked up to the receptionist and asked: "Is Giulia Melucci in?"

"I'm Giulia Melucci," I said.

Kit, who later purported to have been infatuated with me from the moment he met me, had forgotten what I looked like when he came to find me. I, in turn, was unaware that I had spent hours with the guy I had been checking out on the elevator. Kit, fresh out of Georgetown, was staying with the Petrianos in New Jersey until he could find his own place in New York. When he landed a job at Atlantic Monthly Press, a small independent publisher whose young, hard-partying editors were often skewered in the pages of *Spy*, Larisa told him his office was right next door to mine. Standing next to the reception desk, he invited me to a party with him and Michael that weekend. I couldn't go—nor did I want to. I could tell Kit was interested in me, ergo I wanted nothing to do with him. But I did notice when I didn't hear from him over the next few months. Then the letter arrived, the day after I moved out of my mother's house, the perfect day for such a letter. "New apartment, new boyfriend." I was ready. I called him right away, and we made a lunch date for that Thursday.

Bizarre, springlike weather had taken hold of New York City that January, so Kit and I picked up lunch at an upscale takeout down the street and ate on a bench in Union Square Park, facing our offices. Kit hardly touched his smoked turkey and Brie on baguette because he talked so much. As he reminisced about college, he made a reference to bongs made out of apples, which put me off a bit—my drug days, however brief, were behind me. This seemed incongruous; Kit appeared the proper young gentleman in every other respect, from his Church's handmade English shoes to his antique cigarette case. I had plenty of time to study him. I finished my split-pea soup, roll, and cookie, and there he was with most of his lunch still in front of him. It made me restless just sitting listening to him talk on and on with no food left. (When I eat and talk simultaneously, neither activity gets neglected.) I was immensely relieved when Kit pulled out a cigarette—finally, something to do with my antsy appendages. I was also pleased that the man who was going to be my boyfriend was a smoker—especially if he was such a slow eater. Kit walked me to the lobby of my building, where he bade me call him. "You call *me*," I said. He called, and we made an evening date for the next week. Kit asked me to meet him at his office; from there we'd go have drinks at nearby Cedar Tavern.

Not only did Kit seem nervous when I picked him up, but he was wearing a pair of jeans that were just awful. They weren't anything so unforgivable as stone-washed—one of the many fashion horrors of the late eighties—but they were a uniform powder blue, which was almost as bad. This didn't make sense, since Kit had exhibited a well-honed sense of style in our previous meetings. The fact that Kit so clearly liked me made him seem vulnerable, and those jeans weren't helping. But at this point, I wanted a relationship enough that I rallied myself to rise above it. Kit was a good man, a gentle and kind man. He was undeniably handsome, he had an excellent build, nice lips, and thick brown hair flecked with blond. He was smart, and he looked it in his horn-rimmed glasses. Powder blue jeans be damned!

Kit's fashion faux pas was further redeemed by his ability to talk about the abstract expressionist painters who made Cedar Tavern their watering hole in the 1950s. I studied art history at college and intended to pursue a higher degree in the discipline, but then I didn't bother to study for the GRE; on the two mornings I was scheduled to take the graduate school entrance exam, I opted to stay in bed instead. It wasn't a bad decision (or lack thereof); I liked the rhythm of office life and the dependable paycheck, however pathetic that paycheck was. (At the time, I was making $12,000 annually.) I was working at one of the coolest places in New York media, which went a long way toward enhancing the terrible wages—a fact my employers were well aware of. Still, I was delighted that Kit brought some of my stifled scholarly leanings back to my day-to-day, and his riffs on the canvases of Mark Rothko and Franz Kline were undeniably alluring.

As Kit and I talked, we found we had something even bigger in common: Both our fathers had died, Kit's just before his high school graduation and mine just before my college graduation. When you lose a parent at an early age, you have an instant feeling of kinship with others who've had the same experience. There's no way you can describe that sort of grief to someone who hasn't yet known it. You can't describe it even to yourself. I was seeing the psychologist about that, too.

Kit complimented me for not making a big deal over the fact that he was from North Dakota, as people often did. It wasn't that I was so worldly; it's just that I was from Brooklyn and had spent all my life in New York. North Dakota, to me, was no different from, say, Ohio—it was just another place that wasn't New York. Kit knew how to hunt and fish, and his father had been a taxidermist. The youngest of four, he was the only one in his family ever to venture east. Drug references continued to pop up in Kit's conversation—there were his own stories of golfing at night on mushrooms or more historical detours on Oscar Wilde's penchant for absinthe. He seemed obsessed with Rimbaud, which I found both romantic and, as I learned more, worrisome.

I had recently sworn off drugs for good after what amounted to a "lost weekend" spent at a genteel house in East Hampton with a group of Brits who were friends of a friend from *Spy*. Amid the cabbage rose–patterned chintz, we ate too many mushrooms, overly eager for the effects to begin. From there I descended into an existential hell, culminating in a bad melodramatic speech on the meaninglessness of it all. I was lost in a dark wood that no amount of puffy sofas could rescue me from. Had someone recorded my monologue, it could have served as an effective primary source for drug-prevention seminars.

But this peculiar circumstance of being on a date with a guy who actually wanted to impress me rather than the other way around, one who peppered his conversation with a plethora of opiate references, was making me want some. Ready to move the evening along, I asked Kit if he had any back at his apartment. Alas, all he had to offer was snuff—powdered tobacco you snort like cocaine. It was an anachronism, part of some sort of American aristocrat persona Kit had adopted to balance out his prairie roots. I pretended that I had always wanted to try snuff. On the way over to Kit's apartment, we picked up some Pringles potato chips (my choice, a childhood taste that lingered) and Coca-Cola for dinner.

I have yet to see another apartment quite as grim as Kit's. It featured a tiny windowless room that was bathroom, kitchen, living room, and home office all in one. Off to the left was a bigger room with a window that appeared to look out onto something other than bricks but was off-limits because it was crammed full of stuff that belonged to the guy Kit was subletting from. There was a minuscule bedroom, not much larger than the size of a twin bed, with a window that looked out onto an air shaft where pigeons gathered and squawked.

Kit had done his best to cheer up the place. The walls were lined with appealingly haphazard decor—a boomerang, a tear sheet of an ad from the 1920s depicting an older man and a younger one on bikes: "Father and son on a chummy run." I tried the snuff, and later that night I tried some other things I hadn't tried before.

"My pillow smells like your perfume," read the hand-delivered note that arrived the next day. No more romantic words have been written to me before or since. I wondered if there might be something off about Kit. He seemed truly smitten with me, and that kind of thing just didn't happen. I can count on my breasts the number of times I have missed a meal, but for several days after that date I ate next to nothing. Picking at a salad on an emergency date-analysis lunch with my roommate, Jen, the next day, I tried to describe Kit. By this time I was in full self-sabotage mode, and it had completely colored my memory of his physical attributes. I found the gooniest-looking guy in the vicinity of the restaurant and pointed to him. "He looks like that," I said.

"No, he doesn't!" Jen, knowing me well, retorted.

"Okay, maybe not so bad, but something like that."

If my own eyes were not to be trusted, I could have been clued in by other events that there was something unforgettable about Kit. Apparently, every woman he had ever known remained hung up on him. When I first started staying at his place, nary a night went by when there wasn't a call from his college girlfriend. (Turned out they were still dating as far as she was concerned, but that's a story for her book.) Even an old high school flame from North Dakota rang in the middle of the night on a weekly basis.

In spite of my anxieties, we became a

couple. Kit, for his part, did nothing to exacerbate them. He left no doubt that he was serious about me. He always called when he said he would. He carried my bag if it was heavy whenever we walked anywhere. He was delighted to take the hourlong train ride to my mother's house in Bay Ridge, even to spend just an hour, if that's where I happened to be on a Saturday evening. In the beginning, the only problems were mine. This introduction to love and sex was frightening to me, so I invented problems to give substance to fears I couldn't understand. For the first month I convinced myself I was pregnant, even though I was hypervigilant about birth control and the chances of this were slim. Then I decided Kit was gay when I lost track of him and his friend Matt at a party. I didn't even have the sense to keep my worries to myself. I brought them all to Kit, who put up with my neuroses like a saint.

Another new world, one less wrought with conflict, was opening to me at this time. That one existed in the kitchen of my new apartment, where a stove and oven of my own brought out a previously unacknowledged desire to cook. The kitchen to which I had recently bade farewell was strictly my mother's domain, filled on Sunday mornings with the perfume of meat frying for the traditional Sunday ragù. As a child I would have a just cooked, perfectly seasoned meatball for breakfast—with bright green parsley peeking out of juicy meat, it tasted even better than the one I'd have that evening in the finished sauce. On weeknights, she might make a lamb stew with baby artichokes and fava beans; baked lemon sole covered in fresh bread crumbs; or—plainer, but no less delicious—roast beef with gravy and mashed potatoes.

My mother, Janet, was first-generation Italian-American born in Brooklyn; my father, Nicola, came from the south of Italy to the States to establish a medical practice. They settled in Brooklyn and had five children: three girls and two boys,

of whom I am the youngest. Despite cli-
chés about the emotional Italian sensibility, my parents did not fling around the
hugs and the I-love-yous. On the other
hand, when they were angry with us, we
knew it. Dad worked hard and Mom fed
us well; those were the main avenues in
which we could discern their love and
commitment to our well-being. When my
father wasn't seeing patients until late in
the evening, elaborate three-course dinners were the rule. At our round kitchen
table, topped with a brightly patterned
fabric tablecloth and matching napkins,
we always began with a pasta dish, followed by meat or fish and a vegetable.
My mother is Sicilian, which to her
means a meal is not complete until you
have "something sweet." She is dogged in
her pursuit of the best desserts and will
drive any distance if she hears there's a
good bakery hidden somewhere in the
tristate area. If she wasn't just back from
one such expedition, she'd whip something up: a coconut custard pie, a choco-

late bundt cake, or moist ricotta fritters covered in powdered sugar.

Having a home to me has always meant food in the refrigerator. My roommate, Jen, and I were on the same page about that. Jen, who is Jewish and grew up in Westchester, loves to eat as much as I do (in fact, I wouldn't be friends with anyone who doesn't), and she can testify to my mother's talents. She still rhapsodizes about the many weekends she spent at my house when we were in college and my father was still alive and my mother cooked phenomenal meals. If we missed dinner because we had been out for a night of drinking or dancing at some Manhattan club, we knew we could count on a cache of leftovers waiting in the refrigerator when we returned. I knew of no other family who ate the way ours did. One night we arrived to find my brother Nick and his friend John already well into the raid.

"What are you having?" I asked them, a little worried that there would be nothing left for us.

"I'm having the swordfish, and Nick's having the chocolate cheesecake," said John, his voice filled with wonderment. He felt he'd discovered gold—I knew it was just what you might find at our house on any given night.

The first evening in our new apartment, after settling our things, Jen and I went out and shopped for groceries at the overpriced "gourmet" store up the street. When we returned, I dropped a bag containing a bottle of extra-virgin olive oil we could scarcely afford. The glass shattered and the oil spilled all over the kitchen floor. Jen grabbed a mop; I called my mother immediately because I knew she would sympathize with this tragedy. It was the first of many calls I would be making to my mother to announce a culinary mishap. Over the years, I have sought her advice on substituting self-rising flour for all-purpose flour (the remedy is on the package); I've asked her how to save homemade gnocchi I removed from the water too soon (they can't be saved) and what to do if the roast needs another hour and my guests have already been sitting around for an hour eating olives and cheese (just keep pouring drinks). My mother would also be receiving more than a few calls about my romantic failures, but she has fewer clear answers to these.

If my mother did not impart to me an understanding of how to play games when it comes to love, she at least sent me into the world with a clear knowledge of how to make a simple tomato sauce. The foods I had seen her prepare countless times were those I made for Kit in the early days of our relationship. Penne with tomato sauce and basil was a typical first course for a Melucci weeknight supper; my mother would always hide a few slices of fried eggplant at the bottom of each bowl as a tasty surprise. The pasta would be followed by breaded veal or chicken cutlets sautéed in olive oil and butter, accompanied by lemon wedges; there was always a salad of romaine lettuce garnished with slices of red onion and chunks of orange. This was the first meal I made on my own. I shared it with Kit.

〰〰〰〰〰〰

Fried Eggplant

1 eggplant (preferably the small Italian kind, if you can find them)
2 tablespoons olive oil
Salt

Slice the eggplant into rounds about 1/4 inch thick.

Heat the olive oil in a skillet, add as many slices of eggplant as will fit comfortably in the pan, and cook until lightly browned on both sides. You may need to add more olive oil if the pan gets dry, since eggplant absorbs a lot of oil.

Remove slices to a plate lined with two paper towels. Sprinkle with salt.

Yield: Enough for 2 and then some.

~~~ ~~~ ~~~ ~~~

Simple Tomato Sauce and Pasta for Two

1 cup whole plum tomatoes (they must be whole plum tomatoes, and they must be from Italy, though I will confess that sometimes, when I feel lazy, I buy the ones that are already chopped; don't tell my mother)

1 tablespoon olive oil, plus a little more for finishing

1 clove garlic, minced (or 2 tablespoons finely chopped onion)

Pinch of hot red pepper flakes (optional here and in all subsequent recipes; I happen to like using them whenever possible)

Basil leaves

1 teaspoon sugar

1/4 cup red wine

1/2 teaspoon salt

1/2 pound penne, or pasta of your choice

Freshly grated parmigiano, pecorino, or any grating cheese to sprinkle on top

Run the tomatoes through a food mill or puree them with an immersion blender (I do the latter), chop them, or just break them up with your hands. Heat the olive oil in a skillet over medium heat, then add the garlic (or onions) along with the red pepper flakes and 1 whole basil leaf. Lower heat (you do not want your base to brown) and sauté until the garlic is lightly golden (or the onions are translucent), 2 to 3 minutes. Add the tomatoes and raise the heat back to medium; when the sauce begins to simmer, add the sugar, wine, and salt. After about 5 minutes, check to see if it needs more salt; if it tastes acidic, add another pinch or two of sugar. Reduce the heat to low and taste after about 15 minutes. When all the flavors are nicely blended, it's done.

Place a large, covered pot filled with water over high heat. When the water has reached a vigorous boil, add a generous dose of salt (salty water is essential to flavorful pasta; it should have the aroma of the Mediterranean). Add the pasta and let the water return to a boil (covering the pot for those few early moments helps; just remember to remove the cover as soon as the water is boiling again), then give the pot a few good stirs. Continue to cook, stirring occasionally, until the pasta is still firm to the bite but no longer chalky (anywhere from 8 to 12 minutes depending on the pasta shape you're using). You should taste it after about 8 minutes to see where it is. You can't time pasta; you can know it's done only by tasting it.

When the pasta is cooked, drain it and put it back in the pot you cooked it in. Then add a ladleful of the sauce, a tiny splash of olive oil, and a few basil leaves torn with your hands. Line two bowls with a few slices of the fried eggplant (you could add whatever is left to a sandwich, maybe with cutlets, if there are any left, for tomorrow's lunch), then add the pasta and garnish the top of each dish with a spoonful of sauce and a few more pieces of basil. Pass the grated cheese at the table.

Yield: 2 servings.

~~~ ~~~ ~~~ ~~~

Breaded Cutlets

   2 eggs, lightly beaten, seasoned with 1/4
      teaspoon salt
   3/4 cup bread crumbs, seasoned with 1/4
      teaspoon salt, freshly ground pepper, and 1
      tablespoon chopped parsley
   1 pound thin veal cutlets (or chicken,
      depending on your mood, politics, or
      pocketbook)
   2 tablespoons olive oil
   1 tablespoon butter
   1 lemon

Put the eggs in a wide-rimmed bowl and
spread the seasoned bread crumbs on a
plate. Coat the meat in the eggs and then
the bread crumbs. In a skillet, heat the
oil and butter at medium-high and fry
the cutlets until they are cooked through
and browned on both sides (about 4 minutes on each side, depending on thickness). You'll probably need to do this in
two batches; refresh the fat in the pan if

necessary. Remove the cutlets to a plate lined with two paper towels until ready to serve. Present them with lemon slices to squeeze on top.

Yield: 2 servings.

~~~ ~~~ ~~~ ~~~

Romaine Salad with Oranges and Red Onion

1 head romaine lettuce
1/2 small red onion, thinly sliced and cut into
   1-inch strips
2 navel oranges
1 tablespoon olive oil
Splash of red wine vinegar
Salt and freshly ground pepper to taste

Wash and dry a head of romaine lettuce and cut the leaves crosswise into 1-inch pieces. Put them in a bowl with room enough for tossing and add the onion. Remove the stem ends of the oranges, then take off the skins with a paring knife. Cut into slices 1/4 inch thick and then cut the slices into quarters, removing any seeds and startlingly obvious white pith. Dress and toss the salad with olive oil, red wine vinegar, a little salt, and freshly ground pepper.

Yield: 4 servings.

We ate sitting on the floor, our dishes perched on a square ottoman that came from my family's house. We were saving up for a table, but, priorities ever in place, we dropped $3 on a bottle of Concha y Toro, purchased at our local liquor store, where the clerk and his merchandise stood behind bulletproof glass and you pointed out what you wanted. The Concha y Toro was positioned front and center, and good thing—you wouldn't want to be forced to do too many elaborate hand gestures to obtain a $3 bottle of wine. It tasted good enough to our undeveloped palates, a fine pairing for that uncomplicated food.

Kit used to say we had a "charmed life" because, though we could barely afford the rent on our apartments, our jobs exposed us to a kind of glamour that belied our checking accounts. One evening, we attended a book party at the home of a famous television newsman. In his luxurious apartment high over Central Park, we sipped champagne and nibbled canapés presented on silver trays. There was smoked salmon on toast points, asparagus wrapped in prosciutto, Gruyère dumplings, and tempura shrimp, but as always happens at these sophisticated fetes, there wasn't quite enough of it. Two hours later we were on the subway, still hungry, with $5 between us to buy dinner. We picked up a box of spaghetti at the corner store and counted on there being some butter in Kit's refrigerator. Better yet, we found four strips of bacon and three eggs—all the makings of a simple carbonara. I got to work at Kit's tiny stove, and the pasta turned out to be a hearty antidote to those precious little snacks. We even had some left over for the next day—and a dollar left until payday, still a week away.

~~～～～～～～～

Spaghetti Carbonara

3 slices bacon, cut into 1/2-inch pieces
12 ounces dry spaghetti
3 eggs
1/4 cup freshly grated pecorino, plus a little
   more for passing
1/4 cup freshly grated parmigiano, plus a little
   more for passing
Salt
Freshly ground pepper

Fry the bacon until it is almost crispy, then drain on a plate lined with paper towels.

Cook the pasta according to the directions on page 32. Meanwhile, in a large heatproof bowl or serving dish, lightly beat the eggs and add the cheeses.

When the pasta is cooked, drain it in a colander and add it to the bowl with the eggs in cheese. Toss the pasta with the egg mixture, letting the eggs cook on the hot pasta (they may not be completely cooked; I like the creaminess of the not-fully-cooked egg, but if you don't like that idea, throw it all in a skillet over low heat and let it cook a little), then add the bacon. Taste and add salt, if needed, and a few grindings of pepper.

Divide the pasta into warmed bowls.

Serves 2, with leftovers.

I was elated every time I made something that turned out well; it seemed to happen so frequently that I was elated a lot! I was discovering a talent I hadn't known I possessed. Kit enjoyed what I made, but he couldn't relate to my excitement. My boyfriend, a man of infinite curiosities, did not count food among them. He could wake up one morning needing to know everything there was to know about Sergei Diaghilev and the Ballets Russes; the next day it might be the Merz collages of Kurt Schwitters. I got secondhand enrichment from his ever changing obsessions but was truly disheartened when he told me that, like his father before him, he wished he could just take a pill for nourishment and be done with it. The news brought home a deep divide between us. I lived to eat. Kit preferred to take in the majority of his calories through alcohol.

I got my first inkling of the problem when I arrived at his apartment early one evening to find him already most of the way through an oil can of Foster's Lager, with another on deck. This seemed like an awful lot of beer, but I didn't say anything—I just tucked away the information, where it popped out from time to time for me to worry about.

Kit got his dream job at *Rolling Stone* magazine right around the time I got laid off from *Spy*—he pulled himself away from his own going-away party to rush over to my apartment with ice cream to cheer me up. Though I didn't do much at *Spy,* I was proud to have a spot on the magazine's masthead. I had worked my way up from receptionist (or "publishing assistant") to photo researcher and then public relations assistant, and although it was fun to call up gossip columns and place items about whatever celebrity the magazine was lambasting that month, what I really wanted to be was an editor. But at twenty-four I believed myself too old to change direction. I immediately got another job in publicity at Kit's old workplace, Atlantic Monthly Press. Anton, one of the editors, called me "Super-Duper" or sometimes just "Super," because when Kit and I first started dating, he asked Kit how his girlfriend was and Kit said, "Superduper!" Everyone there thought Kit and I were adorable—but not so adorable that I didn't get laid off yet again when Atlantic was sold less than a year into my tenure.

The difficult economy of the early nineties was taking its toll on my career. Meanwhile, Kit was thriving at *Rolling Stone*, where his responsibilities included babysitting his idol, Hunter S. Thompson, the magazine's national affairs editor, when-

ever he came to town. That job entailed ordering pitchers of Bloody Marys for "King
Gonzo" to drink while he had his bath at
the Carlyle Hotel or picking up a cocaine
supply from his dealer. Kit was in heaven;
he talked about Hunter incessantly, mostly
to my acute boredom. I got another publicity job at another publisher, where my
work consisted of promoting authors as
lofty as Edna O'Brien and as lowbrow as
Joan Collins, neither of whom ever asked
me to get them drugs—though once Joan
Collins tried to get me to cancel one of her
book signings at a Costco because there
were "fat people" there.

The spring after Kit and I started dating,
my mother sold the house in Bay Ridge,
moved into a nearby apartment, and bought
another house on the Long Island Sound in
Connecticut—a house where her sister, my
aunt Marie, who never married and worked
in Greenwich, could live full-time and all of
us could gather on holidays. I never really
liked the Connecticut house all that much;
it could never compare with the one we

had. Losing that place truly finalized the loss of my father. Kit was there with me as I took in the sight of those empty halls, their parquet floors clouded with the dust from magnificent old carpets that were taken away and put into storage. He knew exactly how I was feeling and helped me carry some of the weight of it.

Still, since our apartments were a little depressing, Kit and I spent many weekends in Connecticut. He never showed up without a bouquet of flowers for my mother, who worshipped him from the moment she heard his voice from her bedroom that first night he came to see me. He clinched his hold on her affections by showing endless enthusiasm for her favorite card game, May I?

Kit and I drove all over Fairfield County, exploring.

One of our greatest finds was a shack of a restaurant even Kit was crazy about called Tacos or What? It was run by a middle-aged hippie and staffed by cute hippie teenage girls; the place always felt slightly unsavory to me, but the burritos were savory enough for me to let it slide. We never did find the house where Scott Fitzgerald (Kit's favorite writer) and his wife, Zelda, lived for a summer on Compo Road in Westport, though we drove up and down that street dozens of times looking for it.

Besides tacos with a special yellow hot sauce only regulars knew about ("the yellow death"), there was one other food that could delight Kit almost as much as gin-soaked olives: bacon. On those weekends, my mother and my aunt and I collaborated on big breakfasts. Aunt Marie made scrambled eggs with perfect curds and just the right hue, and my mother baked blueberry muffins dipped in melted butter and dusted with sugar, a recipe of her mother's. Kit took care of the bacon preparation, while I assisted.

～～ ～～ ～～ ～～

Nana's Blueberry Muffins

Butter, softened, for greasing muffin tins

1 3/4 cups self-rising flour
1/4 cup sugar
1/4 cup milk
6 tablespoons melted butter
1 egg
1 cup blueberries
1 tablespoon butter (optional)
1/4 cup sugar (optional)

Preheat oven to 400 degrees. Butter muffin tins.

Mix flour and sugar, stir in the wet ingredients, then add the blueberries. Spoon batter into muffin tins, filling each cup about three-quarters full. Bake for 15 to 20 minutes. Cool in pan for 10 minutes, then remove to a cooling rack.

While the muffins are still a little warm, melt 1 tablespoon butter and pour it onto a saucer. Place 1/4 cup sugar on another saucer. Dip the muffins in the butter, then the sugar. This step is optional, but I highly recommend it.

Yield: 9 muffins; recipe can be doubled.

The Lower East Side we inhabited was a far cry from what it is today. To get from my apartment on Avenue A to Kit's on Avenue B, we had to walk through Tompkins Square Park, then a "tent city" inhabited by the homeless. My block was a drug thoroughfare, which, ironically, kept it safe. (The drug dealers saw to it that no muggings occurred, thus keeping police attention away from their territory.) Kit's block was so remote that even the drug dealers stayed away; he was mugged a few times. One day while riding the subway together and grumbling about our living situations, out of the blue I suggested we find a place together in Brooklyn. He agreed with instant and effusive eagerness. With Kit, the big things were easy. We began our apartment search.

"I want to live here with you. I want to make you stews," said Kit in the most adorable voice as we were driving around Boerum Hill, the Brooklyn neighborhood where we hoped to find a place to rent. He was a little tanked. The only time he ever cooked for me was after the first night I slept over at his place. That morning, he fried up bacon and scrambled eggs in the fat left behind. I cleaned my plate, then griped about how full I was and how fat I felt. When I later reminded Kit about the stews he promised, he told me that he would never cook for me again because the one time he tried all I did was complain. I don't know any woman who would have felt differently after those eggs, but maybe I could have hidden it better. Still, I may have been a bit of a battle-ax in the first blushes of our love, but I deserved forgiveness—and maybe even a little stew.

That was probably the only jerky thing Kit ever said to me, and he said it stone-cold sober; Kit was an absolute sweetheart when he was drunk. Which left me confused about the extent of his problem. Don't alcoholics yell and slap you around when they've had a few too many? Kit wasn't like that at all. He would tell me I was beautiful (he did that even without alcohol). He'd say he wanted to crawl into the little scar above my right eyebrow and live there for the rest of his life.

Instead, we moved into the second floor of a one-hundred-year-old brownstone on one of the prettiest blocks in Brooklyn. The place was positively cheery, with big windows that looked out on trees and let in an abundance of light. It had two marble fireplaces (one even worked), the floors were dark wood, and the walls retained their original carvings and cornices. The enormous bathroom had a pedestal sink, an old-fashioned claw-footed tub, and wood wainscoting. Alas, the only thing that wasn't wonderful about that apartment was the kitchen. It consisted of a few slapdash cabinets, a small electric stove, and a noisy refrigerator placed in a corner of the living room.

With little money to spend, we outfitted that sorry space with bottom-of-the-line pieces from Ikea. A set of "camping cookware" set us back $10, but it had everything I needed: a big pot to boil pasta, a small skillet to make sauce, and two saucepans, one big and one smaller. A six-piece knife set with a block cost twelve bucks. I was, in effect, cooking with toys, but I managed to conjure up fantastic meals on my crap stove. I learned that you do not need fancy cookware and a restaurant-grade range to make delicious food; the only true essentials to good cooking are fine ingredients and a sense of how to use them. This you get from cooking on your own, watching others, and eating as many different types of food and preparations as you can. Other than that, the only absolute necessity is a heat source and something heatproof to put your ingredients in: nothing much more sophisticated than what our ancestors came up with in their caves.

Even with just twelve inches of counter space, living together—to me—meant a serious commitment to making dinner. I called Kit every afternoon to get his thoughts on what we might have. He could not have been less interested in these discussions. Kit's mother, Dolores, met the same resistance I did in getting her son to care about food. Every month she mailed him a box of homemade rhubarb sticky buns or chocolate-chip cookies. He never touched them—so I did, unable to bear the thought of that woman's efforts going to waste. Kit arrived in New York with a potato masher and a little spiral notebook filled with his mother's recipes written in her perfect cursive. He liked when I made her meat loaf, though I was a bit skeptical at first. The ingredients Dolores listed did not alarm me—my own mother used onion soup mix in her meat loaf—but I was put off by her direction to "frost" it with ketchup and mustard. I tried to eliminate that step, but Kit insisted I make it exactly the way "Mama Fraser" had written it. I gave in, and the mixture made a thick coating that I had to admit was kind of tasty.

Dolores Fraser's Meat Loaf

2 pounds ground beef

1 envelope onion soup mix

3/4 cup bread crumbs

3/4 cup water

1/3 cup ketchup

Oil or butter for greasing

2 tablespoons ketchup

2 tablespoons mustard

Preheat oven to 350 degrees.

Combine the first five ingredients in a medium bowl and mix well with your hands. Form into a loaf and bake in a 13 by 9-inch baking or roasting pan greased with some oil or butter. Frost with 2 tablespoons ketchup mixed with 2 tablespoons mustard.

Bake for 1 hour. Don't be alarmed by the fact that the meat loaf will be red when you take it out of the oven: That's only the frosting; it's done.

Serves 4 to 6.

Confident that I could cook for two, I was ready to up the numbers. Kit and I invited new friends from work and old friends from school to dinner parties. Though our expandable Ikea table was a far cry from my mother's dining room set, I took the same care she did setting the table. I had one of her many sets of silver, this one mysteriously devoid of soup spoons, which was fine at the time; I wasn't ready to make soups. There were eight place settings of china my grandmother, long dead, had won years before at a benefit luncheon for a charity she was involved in that helped struggling Italian immigrants (as if there were any of those by 1970). The downside of these otherwise delightful dinner gatherings was my increasing awareness of Kit's ability to seemingly drink as much as our other guests—combined. He was a gracious host, a witty toastmaster, and a burgeoning master mixologist—or, as I interpreted these things, an alcoholic. I confronted Kit; I was concerned for him,

and for us. Kit denied that he was anything other than a guy who liked to have
a good time, but it was becoming abun-
dantly clear that his relationship with alcohol—and subsequently me—was anything but good.

Living together magnified our differ-
ences. I was ready to settle into a domestic routine. Kit had other things he
wanted to do with his life, primarily having to do with drinking. Just about every weekend he had a bar crawl planned
with Joe, John, or some guy known simply as Clam. These typically lasted until
the early morning. If I wanted to go out
on a Friday or Saturday, I had to make my
own plans. One Friday evening in spring,
I went to the market and picked up fresh
asparagus to sauté in white wine and
garlic and serve over angel-hair pasta. I
made the sauce, put the water up to boil,
and waited; Kit never came home. Eventually I ate the pasta alone. Kit had decided to join a poker game at the office,
after which the players toured the bars

of Midtown; then Kit came home with a Budweiser tall boy to drink before going to bed at four a.m.

～～～～～～～

Angel-Hair Pasta with Asparagus

  1 pound asparagus (the thinnest kind
    available)
  2 tablespoons olive oil
  Pinch of hot red pepper flakes
  1 clove garlic, sliced thinly
  1 teaspoon salt
  1/2 cup white wine
  1/2 pound angel-hair pasta
  Freshly grated parmigiano or pecorino
  Freshly ground pepper

Wash asparagus and use only the tenderest parts. You can determine which those are by breaking each stalk with your hands. The tough fibers will separate at exactly the right place all on their own. Cut the remains diagonally into 1-inch pieces.

Warm the olive oil over medium heat,

then add the red pepper flakes and garlic. Sauté until the garlic is golden, then add the asparagus and coat with the olive oil. Add salt, cook for 5 minutes, then add the wine and cook for another 10 minutes or until the asparagus has softened to your liking.

Cook the pasta according to the directions on page 32, stirring often; angel hair is particularly vulnerable to knots. When the pasta is done, drain it in a colander and add it to the skillet with the asparagus. Stir and cook over a low heat for about 20 seconds, then serve in warmed bowls. Sprinkle with cheese and freshly ground pepper, if desired.

Serves 2 but will be eaten alone.

Fed up with eating at home by myself, I enrolled in a free culinary education funded by the seemingly unlimited expense account of my friend and former colleague Deborah Kwan. Deborah was the daughter of Chinese immigrants who owned a restaurant in San Francisco; her interest in and love of food was deep, like mine, and tied to family. Deborah worked at a publishing house that seemed to throw the money around, and we went somewhere fabulous nearly every night on the company dime—we enjoyed simple bistro cooking at the Odeon or savored complex and delicate flavors at Bouley. We ate at new places, old places, culinary shrines, and tourist traps. We held the line for ages to get a coveted reservation and waited at the bar forever at any first-come-first-served establishment we deemed worthy. Deborah left publishing to pursue a career in the kitchen, and from there the gravy train only got richer. After a short course at Peter Kump's, she became a pastry chef at 44, the restaurant at the Royalton Hotel, famous at the time for being the ad hoc cafeteria for all the big magazine editors: Anna Wintour, Graydon Carter, and Tina Brown lunched at the prime booths every afternoon. Deborah fell in love with the sous chef (whom she eventually married), and when she wasn't on duty we would eat at the restaurant. We didn't have to order a thing; we just sat back while Erik sent up plate after plate of brilliant food, for which we would be charged next to nothing. A Kump's classmate of Deborah's went to work in the pastry kitchen of Le Cirque, and we ended up there one night with a bottle of champagne and an array of sixteen stunningly beautiful desserts before us, including a chocolate stove with a marzipan skillet full of strawberry sauce atop it (the waiter sang a little song before he dumped that skillet's contents over the stove), Grand Marnier soufflé, chocolate pots de crème, and a tower of tiny ice-cream cones, each a different flavor. These excursions served as finishing school for me—they educated my palate, informed my understanding of food, and made me a better cook.

No matter how many sorbets, gelées, or beignets I was presented with on a given night, my expeditions never went on as long as Kit's. In the early days of our cohabitation, I waited up, worried about him traveling on the subway to our "emerging neighborhood" at four, five, even seven in the morning. Even the neighborhood watch patrol of local residents who walked up the block in reflective shells had called it quits by then. Eventually, as Kit's nights on the town became more and more frequent, I stopped worrying and just went to bed. Eventually, instead of relief, I felt annoyance when he finally came in the door. One night I was awakened by the sound of Kit making dinner after a night of drinking. Here is his recipe.

~~~ ~~~ ~~~ ~~~

Kit's Drunken Soup

Open can of Progresso chicken noodle soup. Put in saucepan over medium heat. Pass out on couch. Cook until girlfriend hears strange crackling sounds and gets out of bed to see what's going on and turns off burner to deal with the mess in the morning.

Time: Usually about 4 hours.

Serves: no one.

I was angry with Kit a lot of the time during the four years we were together, and not only because of his drinking. Whatever it was that kept me away from men for so long continued to linger and do its thing to prevent me from getting too close to Kit. Kit's nocturnal escapades seemed to perform a similar function for him. Still, I was never fully convinced that Kit's drinking was as big a problem as it actually was. I always allowed that I might be blowing his indulgence out of proportion in order to create another barrier. There I was wrong. Though my perception of Kit throughout the four years we were together remained as distorted as it was the day after our first date, when it came to putting distance between us, he met me halfway.

One night while we were both in bed asleep, we were startled by a terrifying crash from the other room. When we ran out to see what had happened, we found that the kitchen cabinets had fallen off the wall. Our collection of dishes—some from Kit's mother, some from my mother, and several from my grandmother—were in pieces all over the floor. The symbolism here escaped neither of us. Not long after that, Kit moved out.

While I never managed to get Kit to value the delicious subtlety of a creamy, perfectly cooked grain of arborio rice, his intellectual fascinations did rub off on me. Together, we grew to be adults, and the things I learned from him—like how Sara Murphy, best friend of Scott and Zelda Fitzgerald and inspiration for Nicole Diver in *Tender Is the Night*, always wore her pearls when she sunbathed on the French Riviera—enhance my cocktail party repertoire to this day. Kit credits me with teaching him how to hail a taxi—essential knowledge for the

burgeoning New Yorker—and for introducing him to his all-time favorite band:
the Jesus and Mary Chain. Kit has since
quit drinking, and he is one of my dearest friends.

~~ ~~ ~~ ~~

My Father

~~ ~~ ~~ ~~

My father was an otorhinolaryngologist, a word I still like to say, even though everyone else goes with the shorter ENT. As a child, I was proud of the fact that my father was a physician and the status it connoted on our family in the days before the invention of HMOs and hedge funds. In first grade, when we were learning the alphabet and I was called on to come up with a word for the letter *V,* I said "vein," which I thought was an awfully smart word to know. In second grade, for show-and-tell, I presented a mounted thirty-two-by-twenty-six-inch diagram of the inner ear borrowed from the wall of my father's office.

That office was in the basement of our house. In the lower left-hand drawer of his big mahogany desk, my father kept a supply of Tootsie Pops, which he offered to the many children whose tonsils he removed. "Would you like strawberry, cherry, grape, or chocolate?" I heard him asking one of them, as I happened past the door to his consulting room, in a soothing tone not often heard by his own children. I envied those kids.

By the time he saw us at the end of the day, my father was usually worn out by the demands of his work and patients. When my brothers and sisters and I were growing up, family dinners could be tense affairs. On the odd evening when a Scotch on the rocks loosened him up, he liked to indulge in the activity that most relaxed him besides golf: the *Reader's Digest* Word Power game. Though Italian was his first language, my father had an English vocabulary that rivaled those of most English literature professors. He never spoke Italian at home, and subsequently we never learned it. (I'm still annoyed about this.) The only time we heard him speak his native language was when dinner was interrupted by a call from an Italian patient whose child had a fish bone caught in his throat or some such dire malady. If we made it through uninterrupted, my father would quiz us afterward with the help of the *Reader's Digest* game, making sure our word skills were up to par. While my mother took care of the dishes, he would sip an espresso or eat a peach cut up and dropped into a glass of red wine, while we ate whatever dessert my mother was offering. I'm sure he appreciated the care she took with our meals, but he never said so, at least not in front of us. He was serious, and there was little light banter between them. He was profoundly interested in our education, and dinner conversations often prompted him to send one of us for the encyclopedia whenever a subject came up that warranted further exploration. He bought us all manner of analog teaching tools. It kills me that he missed the Internet completely; how he would have loved it, especially Wikipedia, which would have saved my brothers and sisters and me countless trips from the kitchen to the library with heavy books in our arms.

If my father revealed affection for us, it was in the smallest ways. On summer evenings after dinner, he took us for walks around the neighborhood to check out the local clothing boutiques; a naturalized American through and through, he was particularly fond of a vintage clothing store, called Lulu's Back in Town, that sold antique Levi's jeans. He enjoyed buying clothes for us and was especially fond of those old jeans with patches made of colorful bandannas stitched onto the knees. When he needed to go to the hospital for evening rounds, he would con one of us into accompanying him with the promise of a stop for ice cream at Carvel, his favorite.

My mother and father went out for dinner by themselves every Wednesday night—his penance for playing golf three days a week. They would go to one of the excellent local Italian restaurants: Tommaso's or Ponte Vecchio. I always wondered what my family-focused parents would have to say to each other at a table without us kids around. My mother always remarked that they were one of the few couples that were always talking, unlike those many sullen ones who just sat across from each other chewing and staring into space, but I never believed her. On Saturdays, they'd go someplace smarter with other couples, usually in "the city." On those nights, my father would spend a longer time than my mother primping in front of the mirror on the door to his closet. He'd try on one tie, then take it off and try another, then he'd decide maybe he should go with a bow tie. My mother would stand by watching, ready to tear out her curly brown hair that had been coiffed hours before.

"I must be the only wife in the world

who waits for her husband to finish dressing before they go out," she would nag.

Because my father grew up in Europe during World War II, when food was scarce, he hated to see anything in our house go to waste. He cooked one thing: minestrone that was born out of his deep fear of food spoilage. Any Saturday that was too wet or cold for golf would find him riffling through the refrigerator, pulling out anything that seemed in peril to put in his soup. No matter what the base, his creation consistently had the same wonderful flavor of tomato, smoky bacon, and vegetables. He always added barley to give it a lovely richness. The most remarkable thing about my father's minestrone was that all the elements were cut with the precision of the surgeon that he was. This I cannot duplicate no matter how I try, but maybe you can.

~~~~~~~~~

My Father's Minestrone

2 slices bacon, cut into 1/4-inch pieces
   (optional)

3 tablespoons olive oil

1 medium onion, chopped

1 shallot, chopped (optional)

3 Yukon gold potatoes (or any white waxy
   potato), cubed

2 small carrots, thinly sliced

2 stalks celery, chopped

1 teaspoon salt, plus extra salt to taste

1 yellow squash, cut into 1/4-inch slices and
   then quartered

1 green squash, cut into 1/4-inch slices and
   then quartered

6 ounces string beans, cut into 3/4-inch pieces

1/2 pound button mushrooms, quartered

4 plum tomatoes, seeded and chopped (or
   1 cup canned whole tomatoes, drained of
   juices and chopped)

1/2 cup corn kernels (drained, if canned)

1 cup fresh or frozen green peas

1 cup canned chickpeas, drained

**1 small head savoy cabbage, outer leaves
removed, chopped**

2 tablespoons butter

1/4 cup barley (or farro) (optional), uncooked

1/4 cup torn basil leaves

1/4 cup chopped parsley

Freshly ground pepper

Freshly grated parmigiano

In a small skillet over medium heat, cook bacon until it takes on a little color and gives off some of its fat. (Whether to add the fat to the soup base or drain it is between you and your Weight Watchers leader. I keep about half of it.) Heat the oil in a large stockpot (8 quarts or more) over heat that is just a notch over medium, then sauté the onion and shallot until they are translucent, about 2 minutes. Add the potatoes, carrots, celery, and 1 teaspoon salt; let the vegetables get a little soft, stirring regularly so they don't stick to the bottom of the pot, about 5 minutes (if it gets too sticky, add a little water). Add squashes, string beans, and mushrooms and continue to stir regularly.

When all the vegetables have softened and the squashes are translucent, add the tomatoes, corn, green peas, and chickpeas, enough water to cover and salt to taste, and cook another 10 minutes, continuing to stir. Then add cabbage and 2 quarts of water, salt to taste, and 2 tablespoons butter. Bring to a simmer, add the barley (if using), then lower heat and cook partially covered for 45 to 50 minutes.

When all the flavors are melded and you're ready to serve, test for salt, add herbs, and serve with ground pepper and freshly grated parmigiano.

Yield: 8 to 10 servings.

During my father's last years, when I was away at school, he and my mother cultivated a new Saturday night ritual. My father made his soup, my mother made a simple pizza from dough bought at a local bakery, then they would rent a 1960s Italian comedy (*Divorce, Italian Style,* starring Marcello Mastroianni, was a particular favorite) and sit in the living room, eating and laughing their heads off. Whenever I spent a weekend at home, I couldn't believe what I was seeing. Where the heck did my parents go? This couple was having fun together. I didn't know them.

At college I studied Italian language and art history; because of this, my relationship with my father grew closer. He was delighted with the interest I took in his native culture and tongue; in the summer between my sophomore and junior years, we traveled to Italy together so I could get to know my aunts, uncles, and cousins in Salerno. On that trip, my father had a hard time walking up the hills of his hometown or up the big marble staircase at the Uffizi Gallery. He had a heart condition; there were tests and medications, but he didn't say much about it, and we didn't ask.

I spent the first semester of my senior year studying in Florence, Italy. The night before I went away, my father and I stayed up late together, ordering sale items from the L.L.Bean catalog (another one of his favorite things). I wanted blue-and-white boxers that were going for $5, but they were available only in size forty-six. "That's fat!" my father said. But never mind, I wanted them and he got them for me. (I used to wear those shorts with a belt. I thought it looked punk.) My father seemed reluctant to part with me that night. I got the feeling that he thought it might be the last time he would ever see me.

From Florence, I wrote my parents long letters describing all the enchanted experiences I was having—more often having to do with a bottle of Brunello and a bowl of ribollita than with Brunelleschi's dome and the sonnets of Petrarch. When I was in Florence, I was sent the most beautiful love note I have yet received. My father wrote it on the back of an envelope containing a card from my mother. Here is what he wrote:

Dearest Giulia,

Mother had already sealed this letter before I had a chance to write anything so I write outside. In fact I am glad to do so, and let everybody see that I think about you and love you very much.

Dad

My father's exacting print was unmistakable, but the sentiment was utterly foreign. I had to read it a few times to make sure it was real.

I had the option to stay in Florence for another semester. I was having the time of my life; I had even developed a crush on a history professor who was engaged but seemed to have real admiration for my thoughts on the hierarchical divisions within the Medici court. I returned to New York because I feared my father would die before the term was up.

It was Christmas when I got back, and our house was filled, as it always was at the holiday, with Bolla wine gift sets and boxes of panettone—gifts from my father's many Italian-American patients. Panettone is a cross between bread and cake, dotted with dried fruits and laced with the scent of sweet liqueur. I never touched it as a child, but in January, when I returned to campus for my last semester, my father sent me off with a couple of bottles of Barbaresco and an enormous panettone in a modernist black-and-red tin. Students with late night munchies will eat just about anything, so my friends and I cut into the panettone one night. Accompanied by the red wine and enhanced by other exotic substances, it wasn't bad. Maybe it was the container, maybe it was the chemicals, but that panettone stayed soft and palatable the entire winter. We had some every night, and we never seemed to make a dent in it. We ate it well into Lent.

The morning after I finished writing my last paper, my father underwent emergency heart surgery. He did not survive the operation. He died three days before my graduation. I still have the envelope with the note he sent me when I was in Florence. It has a permanent place on top of my box of letters. I pick it up and read it every now and then to remind myself of love's many surprises.

I do not have a recipe for panettone. For the past few years, I have scoured the bakeries of Little Italy and the upscale patisseries of the Upper East Side to find a cake as delicious as the one my father sent me to school with that year. I pick up a few each holiday season and eat a piece every morning (and occasionally evening) of the week between Christmas and New Year's Day. Sometimes I'm disappointed with what I've brought home, other times I'm quite pleased. I still haven't found one that's perfect. It's possible that I never will.

The Victory Breakfast

I was cocky when I broke up with Kit. For no good reason, I imagined that the long dateless slog I had endured from birth to the age of twenty-three was well behind me. Kit, on the other hand, was quick to get into a new relationship, though from what I gathered it had a sort of *Who's Afraid of Virginia Woolf?* dynamic. It took longer for me to find the George to my Martha. In those lonely years, whenever I felt sad and uninterested in food, I made myself pastina. Pastina, tiny pasta stars, is Italian baby food, or "baby's first solid food," as the Ronzoni box says. My mother used to make this for me when I was a baby or whenever I was sick as a little girl. I always keep a box of pastina in the house for whenever I'm not feeling quite right or not up to cooking. It is fast, simple, and terribly comforting.

~~~ ~~~ ~~~ ~~~

Pastina

1/4 cup pastina
1/4 teaspoon salt
1 egg, lightly beaten
1 teaspoon butter
1 tablespoon freshly grated parmigiano
Freshly ground pepper

Bring 1 cup of water to a boil in a small saucepan, add pastina and salt, and cook until most of the water is absorbed, 3 to 4 minutes. Turn off heat and add the egg, letting it cook on the hot pasta, then add the butter, cheese, and a little pepper.

Serves 1.

When you're single, the highs are high and the lows are low. You have opportunities for more excitement and pleasure than any person in a committed relationship is ever going to have, and you may as well enjoy them as much as you can because the rug gets pulled out from under you while you still think you're riding high. And before all the married people start slamming this book shut, I will concede that marriage might very well be as much of a blast, I just haven't had the opportunity to find out. What I do know is that the vicissitudes of dating get boring, or you get too old to partake of them, as I have, or both, and you crave the stability of a permanent partnership. I've been craving it for a while now; it just hasn't craved me.

The four years that came between Kit and my next stable relationship included a lot of false starts—exciting beginnings, uncertain middles, and crushing ends, all occurring in the span of a week or two. I took the abrupt endings hard, but

I adored the initial rush. I didn't cook much in those years—on the rare occasions that I did make something for myself, my friends, or a date, I'd think, Oh, I remember when I used to do this, I'm good at this—but mostly I dined out.

I got sad about Kit on a regular basis.

Ginia bore the brunt of it. She was the friend of a friend of a not-very-close college friend. We got to know each other at a party in a Brooklyn backyard on a summer night in 1989. Ginia, an aspiring journalist, was working at a now defunct environmental magazine called *Garbage* at a time when recycling was just a glimmer in Al Gore's eye. We didn't bond until a few years later when Ginia was at *Time* magazine writing the "People" page and I was a publicist at Penguin, desperate to get press for a party celebrating the publication of Robin Leach's *The Lifestyles of the Rich and Famous Cookbook*, a culinary atrocity featuring recipes by Kenny Rogers and Vanna White that I, by some stroke of bad fortune, had been assigned to promote. In the days beforehand, my boss and I panicked over how to deal with the arrivals of the recently separated Ivana and Donald Trump. Our worries were unwarranted, for neither showed up, but getting a *Time* writer there was a feather in my cap. As lovely as the flowing Taittinger champagne was, I couldn't wait to get out. I grabbed Ginia and we beat it over to Trader Vic's, a Polynesian theme bar in the Plaza Hotel, where I imagined prep school boys plied their dates with sweet drinks in the 1950s and that sadly no longer exists. Amid the tikis and lei-adorned waiters, Ginia and I drank mai tais and talked for hours. I was still living with Kit, and I opened up to her about his possible alcohol problem as I drank an impressive quantity of rum punch. She confessed to me her crush on Brad Meyerson, a friend who didn't say much—not about his soon-to-be-revealed devotion to her or, for that matter, anything at all.

Since that night, Ginia's been my best

friend. We have a lot in common: Her father was from Italy and was a sharp dresser like my own. Her mother was born in the States of parents from Sicily, again, just like mine. People even say we look alike. We can share conversation on the New York media world as well as memories of Christmas cassatas. But most of all, we like to talk about dating. Ginia's married now, so she has less to offer on that front. I manage to keep up the flow of stories. She, too, is a brilliant cook who has served me a plethora of delicious meals while listening to tales of my many romantic peaks and valleys.

The first one she had to live through was Serge, a Croatian translator I met on a book tour. As I sat in her Park Slope living room and she served me polenta with mushrooms and Gorgonzola, I explained to her how he was my *passione grande*. I had convinced myself of this. I had to; he started talking about marriage instantly, and those were words I was dying to hear, especially because Kit never mentioned them. I wanted Kit to want to marry me, even though I was pretty sure marrying him was a bad idea. But after two months with Serge, I realized I couldn't bear the sight of him, partially because he found fault with the mildew on my shower curtain while he himself was squatting in a mouse-infested apartment on the Upper East Side, but mostly because I was still in love with Kit. I cried most of the time I was with Serge; I cried when we were in bed, I cried at Barneys when Neil Young's "Harvest Moon" came on while we were shirt shopping (Kit and I used to listen to that album on drives up to Connecticut). I lost it, ran out of the store, and went home alone.

On the heels of that, I got into a long-distance relationship with a friend of a friend from Chicago. It began with a snappy phone rapport established while I was still with Kit. When Tim visited New York, we discovered a sexual rapport as good as the one we had on the phone. I was hesitant to get into a relationship that involved plane travel, but Tim pushed for it, leaving me phone messages with convincing pleas like "To kiss you again would be my privilege." That got me, but things went south as soon as I began to fly west, which I did most of the time, because Tim was afraid of flying.

I dated a Rhode Island WASP who never ate when we went out. "I like to keep my edge," he explained. Less concerned with being dull than with being hungry, I would eat before seeing him, since we usually met well after dinnertime anyway. He resembled a J.Crew model and had slept with half the women in publishing. One morning when I woke up at his apartment, the phone rang; when he finished the conversation, he told me I had to leave because some woman—whom "I could meet someday but not today"—had no hot water and needed to come over to take a shower. I decided that today—not someday—would be the end of us.

There was a summer romance with a

much younger neocon who at twenty-one was writing op-ed pieces for *The Wall Street Journal.* He took a lot of drugs for a conservative, but he was frightfully intelligent. He'd FedEx twenty-page love letters from his downtown office to my uptown office. I wish I had kept them, but I didn't because they were sort of creepy. In them he reported his dreams of me, one of which had me clicking my heels three times and getting swept away in ecstasy. I broke up with him when he had to go back to the University of Chicago for one more semester, a fact he had neglected to mention while we were seeing each other. He wrote a last note about an injured deer he saw on the side of the road. He and his friends stopped and tried to help it, but it had to be put down. He compared that violence with the required action he needed to take with his love for me.

I became convinced I would marry a satirical writer from a wealthy family—who resembled the teenage David Helfgott, the mentally ill piano prodigy, or at least the actor who played him (not Geoffrey Rush, but the younger one) in the movie *Shine*—from the moment our blind date was scheduled, a month before we were to meet. I became so obsessed with this man and with getting everything right on the date that I actually had a telephone consultation with one of the authors of *The Rules,* the phenomenally successful dating guide based on fifties-era wisdom. I got this privilege for free from a friend who was the publicist for the book. Then the night I met him, I broke the cardinal rule. I slept with him, and it played out just the way those yentas predicted it would.

I went on a few dates with a guy whose last name I never caught, who after the third date left me a message announcing that he was going out of town forever. This seemed like an unnecessary nicety.

Though my cooking had slowed down outside of relationships and domesticity, I was keeping up with my eating. There is one treat in particular that evokes for me the more upbeat moments of those years. It's something I call the Victory Breakfast.

Even if I wanted to make it for myself, I wouldn't be able to: I'm much too hung over. No, the Victory Breakfast is best prepared at a New York deli or coffee shop; it is the bacon, egg, and cheese on a roll that many urbanites have every morning. I allow myself such a decadent treat only rarely. In those years of delayed adolescence, it was what I ate the morning after a fun night out, followed by a make-out session with a sexy but unavailable guy, preferably accompanied by one hundred cigarettes.

The Victory Breakfast is just the thing to settle the stomach after such a night. The name came to my mind while I was waiting on the preparation of one the morning after a long night spent with a dashing war reporter whose novel I was promoting. Ian and I met for drinks to talk about business one August evening. He lived around the corner from me, so we met at the bar down the street, an old Victorian wood-paneled room with lots of long mirrors and carved wood. I wore a similarly gothic Cynthia Rowley skirt, a yellow damask mini, with a white tank top and matching cardigan slung around my neck.

Ian was holding a bar stool for me when I showed up for our seven o'clock meeting promptly at 7:05. We ordered two pints of Brooklyn Lager. Ian smoked like a madman, and at the time, I smoked like a madwoman whenever I was sitting at a bar with a guy who smoked. Ian told hilarious stories of his stepmother, who had been promoted from nurse to wife after his mother's death but continued to call her husband "boss." He had a strange fascination with the details of Mussolini's execution; and he had seen war and suffering and had taken risks. As we drank beer after beer after beer, I went through the few cigarettes I had on me, then moved to his manly Winstons. Until two in the morning we glided away on nicotine, hops, and conversation. I hadn't eaten a crumb, neither had Ian, and seeing as there was nowhere to get dinner at that hour, I invited him to my apartment for, what do you think?

I hadn't lost touch with myself so much that my pantry didn't contain a few cans of Italian tomatoes and boxes of pasta, various brands: De Cecco, purchased on days I felt flush; Barilla, purchased on the days I felt broke; even one or two boxes of Ronzoni that must have been on some big sale. I always had a hunk of parmigiano in the refrigerator and a few bottles of wine on a rack over the sink. I pulled out a red and poured Ian and myself a glass (as if we really needed to drink more).

We ate the pasta in the little dining nook I had created in a niche in my apartment. Ian had seconds. Did he know those strands had strings attached? Back on the sofa, I made my move: "It's four in the morning and you're on my couch, when are we going to make out?" I asked.

Ian was a gentleman, so he complied a bit, but he had a girlfriend, he told me, and he promised her he wouldn't cheat. (I don't know if I would trust a guy who promised he wouldn't cheat, but that wasn't my problem.) Ian didn't cheat, he managed me and my expectations with grace, somehow leaving intact the brazen confidence that inspired such a bold remark from me.

It wasn't the first time—or, sadly, the last—I was to use such an aggressive come-on. Before Kit, I remained unkissed at the end of nearly every evening I spent with a man who interested me, and in college my friends got tired of hearing me gripe about getting nowhere with every guy I liked. When I found myself alone with Elliot Goldkind, a budding composer and one of the few great-looking straight guys on campus, I couldn't let the opportunity pass without trying something. We had stolen a bottle of wine from a college-sponsored cocktail party and went back to his dorm room, where we talked and laughed about our shared deviance for hours. I was sitting on his bed, and he was sitting at his desk chair, and I just couldn't leave his room without having more to report. "My friends are going to kill me if I don't make out with you," I said somewhere around four in the morning. Elliot didn't take that line with as much sportsmanship as Ian had a similar one so many years later. He told me I had ruined the fun night we were having.

When kinder, gentler Ian left, I dealt with the dishes and got to bed at around five-thirty in the morning. Soon enough, it was time to get up and get dressed for work. I didn't feel tired at all; I was too excited about my night. As I waited in line for my sandwich at the Honey Bee deli across the street from my office, the name came to me: the Victory Breakfast, a tasty reward for a battle hard won. Not long after I consumed that sandwich, I called Ginia to tell her about my night. She was as impressed with my brashness as I was. Right after I hung up with her,

Ian called to say he had a great time. I wondered if he even remembered the kissing part.

I was on a streak. When another writer came over for a dinner party at my house and then stayed after all the guests had left, I figured he wasn't hanging around to help with the dishes, so I recycled the "It's four in the morning" line. Henry didn't have a girlfriend, so it worked better this time, but he wasn't really interested in me, he just knew (from me) that I had kissed Ian and felt he wasn't getting the full complement of publicist services. I didn't care; I couldn't get over the fact that men were interested in my body back then. I had had enough of their interest in my mind, which left me unsatisfied 100 percent of the time. But that all came to an end when I finally got together with Ethan.

The Ethan Binder School of Cooking

I knew quite a bit about Ethan before we started dating. I possessed sufficient information to drive a sensible girl away, but it only propelled me in his direction, which also happened to be where the kitchen was.

There was the fact that it took me nine months and about twenty-seven meals to win him, and then there was his history with Anne, a good friend of mine who dated him for seven years; during four of them they lived together. They had been broken up for three years by the time we met.

I became friends with Anne in the summer of 1997 when we were both part of a group that shared a summerhouse on Shelter Island. Anne wasn't working at the time, so she'd stay at the house all week, and when we arrived on Friday she'd leave little vases of fresh-picked flowers beside every bed. We became instant friends. She is one of the funniest people I know because she isn't afraid to talk about anything. She also happens to be an incredibly imaginative cook. She will play with ingredients I would never have thought of putting together, like black beans with ginger and curry as a dip for tortilla chips, something she calls Jaipur nachos.

Anne was still hung up on Ethan that summer, and he hadn't quite let go of her, either. One of Ethan's friends, Stacey, was also in our house, and Anne would grill her about Ethan from time to time. Since gossip was a sport even more popular than swimming and tennis with this group, everyone listened in and offered theories about Ethan, who was now dating a significantly younger woman. I, too, listened in on these conversations, not one to refrain from participation in the amateur psycho-analyzing of a difficult man, even one I didn't know.

I never expected to fall for Ethan. I didn't even expect to meet him, but the following January, after an afternoon of sofa shopping, Anne and I stopped off for an early evening drink at a West Village café and there he was, sitting at the bar with his friend Perry. So this was Ethan, object of fixation to my dear friend. Why was it that he looked exactly like the man *I* had been looking for, ever since I started looking for a man?

I trace my penchant for smart Jewish guys to the age of twelve, when I found myself fantasizing about Jeff Goldblum, who at the time was costar of a short-lived detective series called *Tenspeed and Brown Shoe.* I wasn't sure where my attraction to his particular look came from, though I suspect it had something to do with an image of repression he radiated. Repressed people draw me like a bubbling tray of lasagna just pulled from the oven—maybe because they give no clues as to what they are thinking, allowing me to project whatever I want on them, sort of like a Rorschach. They also tend to be quite hilarious.

Ethan is the most brilliantly witty man I have ever known. He pinpointed everything that was amusing about people, and we happened to know a lot of the same ones, so we fell into an easy banter when I finally got to talk to him that evening, after putting in twenty minutes or so with Perry pretending to care about the plot of *Little Dieter Needs to Fly*, a film his documentary club, which was currently concentrating on the work of Werner Herzog, had just seen.

Ethan had green eyes the size and shape of almonds that blinked behind narrow glasses. Beneath them was a substantial nose housing formidable nostrils. It may not sound like it from these details, but he was incredibly good-looking. The package worked, even if this description doesn't exactly capture that.

My attraction to him manifested itself as rambunctiousness. I verbally assassinated this magazine editor or that television writer in our shared circle. I made Ethan laugh with the ridiculous things that came out of my mouth. I couldn't resist singing "Detroit Rock City," a Kiss song, any time he referenced his hometown. Inspired by my silliness, Ethan allowed his piercing wit and intelligence to peek out from behind his placid exterior. He had been an editor at *The New Yorker* and a writer for *Rolling Stone;* at the time, he was producing and writing a show for MTV. Most young men in New York City would think these credentials made them the hottest thing to come down the pike, but because Ethan took his achievements in stride, he actually was.

Ethan was looking at me, not past me the way most of the men of my set did. He seemed interested in what I had to say and not just in his own reflected glory. He had made his way around the

New York media orbit, but Ethan was more interested in other subjects, history mainly; he read Barbara Tuchman and Pat Barker. He was passionate about music. He played guitar and had been in several bands in his twenties, then gave up his rock star ambitions to become a writer. I never applied myself to the piano or guitar lessons I took as a child, but I'm a decent singer with excellent pitch and an encyclopedic knowledge of the lyrics to just about every rock and roll song written between 1968 and 1990. Ethan still played for fun with a group of friends every now and then. I knew from Anne where his musical tastes lay; they were the same as hers, which were the same as mine. Without a drop of irony, we listened to 1970s bands like ELO and Chicago, and we liked much from the current scene, postmodern bands like Pavement and Teenage Fanclub.

I also already knew Ethan was into food. After that short meeting I concluded, not incorrectly, that he was the love of my life.

I saw him again just a few weeks later at a dinner party hosted by Stacey from the summerhouse. Stacey is an heiress and definitely not a cook, so she had the meal catered by the Second Avenue Deli. The menu featured brisket and kugel and cheese blintzes; Ethan was seated next to me and told me he was impressed that I knew my way around this spread. I adored these foods and had grown up with them as much as I had the foods of my own tradition. My mother was raised in a Jewish neighborhood and has always had a thing for Jewish ethnic fare. She would often venture back to her old turf to buy layer cakes at Stern's for our birthdays. She'd go to Weinstein's on Avenue U for our annual New Year's Day get-up-late-and-hang-around-all-day-in-your-pajamas larder. There'd be smoked salmon and bagels for breakfast and kosher hot dogs with knishes to eat for the rest of the day, along with the traditional Italian lentils my mother would insist we have "at least a spoonful" of for good luck in the coming year. Our pantry contained nearly as many Manischewitz products as it did Progresso, and it was not unusual for her to make us potato latkes or matzo-ball soup.

I felt really comfortable sitting next to Ethan that evening. He was as enthusiastic a diner as I was and an even funnier dinner partner. We laughed at Stacey's German boyfriend, a film producer of dubious promise who dismissed the meal in a thick German accent, explaining that the couple really preferred to eat "small, healthy dishes." I wanted to be Ethan's Jewish wife and feed him these large, fattening dishes on a regular basis. I got the feeling that Stacey thought we'd be a good match, too. "Do you know that he got a perfect score on his LSAT but decided not to go to law school?" she told me when we were alone together with the dishes. As if I needed any further reason to want Ethan.

But there was something deeper that attracted me to Ethan. Something in him that cried out "Take care of me" in a voice tempered with wariness. He presented a challenge that was tailor-made for me: There was Ethan's wall and my determination to bust through it—a perfect pairing.

Our first date was Valentine's Day. I asked *him* out, selling it as an "anti-Valentine's Day date," though for me that couldn't have been further from the truth. The idea came to me at work one morning (where sheer boredom allowed me to get inventive with my personal life). Anne, who had just started dating a Buddhist poet she was pretty into (whom Ginia later dated to the same counternirvana result), bestowed her blessings upon my idea. A few hours later, I was out to lunch with Kit of all people; as we were crossing Sixth Avenue, *bingo,* we ran into Ethan. I took this as a sign that God too endorsed my plan, so I came right out with it.

"Ethan! So weird running into you, I was just thinking about you," I squealed.

"Really, what were you thinking?" he replied cautiously.

"Well, Saturday is Valentine's Day and you don't have a girlfriend and I don't have a boyfriend and all our friends do. We should go out together so we don't end up at home alone like big losers."

"I'll consider that," Ethan said. "I'll give you a call."

Over sushi, Kit gave it to me straight: To his male eye, Ethan could not have appeared less interested. I later discovered that Ethan had a gift for allowing others to interpret his moods and reactions rather than actively making them known. Kit saw what he was inclined to see, and so did I; I protested that Ethan had been delighted by my invitation. My reading turned out to be accurate: Ethan called the next morning to say he did indeed want to have dinner with me on Saturday.

We decided to go to the Red Rose, an old-school Italian restaurant, one of the last vestiges of the Italian-American working class that were being priced out of our neighborhood. Walking down chronically run-down Smith Street, where a recently opened French bistro and handbag boutique sparked hope of renewal in the hearts of the locals, Ethan sneered: "A restaurant and a bag store does not make a revival." I found his cynicism amusing, but frankly, I was excited about the French bistro and bag store. I made us stop to look in Patois, which was packed with couples eating a better meal than we were going to get at the Red Rose. When we got there and took our seats, I was embarrassed, and not just because the waiter offered us a bottle of red wine with pink hearts on the label. Now that I had Ethan where I wanted him, my confidence left me. I couldn't think of anything remotely enthralling to say, or even anything bland, for that matter; this wasn't the first time I'd found myself tongue-tied on a date.

Throughout high school, I'd harbored an obsessive infatuation with Doug Olivieri, the brother of my sister Carla's boyfriend. Doug was four years older than me and went to New York University. I would show up uninvited at his dorm or call him to talk about the U2 concert I had just seen and keep him on the phone for hours (this was in the early days of the band, mind you; they were pretty cool then). Doug was the first love interest I ever cooked for; I would grill him up a hamburger from the package of frozen patties my mother always kept in the freezer, chatting all the while. Doug was terribly fond of those hamburgers, but he wasn't really interested in me. (Though, come to think about it, there is no other way to explain why he was always coming over; those hamburgers weren't all *that* good.) When I asked him to take me to my senior prom, he agreed. I could barely believe I would have the opportunity to show my classmates that the guy I had been talking about incessantly for the past four years actually existed. In the weeks leading up to the day, I performed regular dress rehearsals, standing in front of my bedroom mirror in my pink vintage dress with sequined bodice and lavender

Christian Dior underwear. But when I saw Doug approaching my front door, corsage box in hand, I froze. When he took my hand at the pre-prom cocktail party in Denise's backyard, I was speechless for the first time in my life. There was nothing I wanted more in the world than to be there with him, but once I was I felt ashamed for wanting it so much. This left me in a rare taciturn moment.

I'd since come up with a way to deal with this affliction when it hit me. I ask questions, making myself seem more like an FBI interrogator than a potential girlfriend. As we dined on mediocre cod mare chiaro and bland chicken rollatini, I found my tongue and interviewed Ethan about his family. He regaled me with stories about his three sisters and their families. He seemed fond of his nieces and nephews and slightly in awe of the hassle his siblings had taken on in the raising of children. "She and her husband toss them back and forth like footballs," he said, describing his youngest, who was in a bit over her head, having given birth to two screamers back-to-back. Ethan's parents had a long, happy marriage. They met at Cornell, where they both studied with Nabokov. His mother was a painter, and the two of them ran an art gallery together. The family home in Detroit contained a teeny tiny Henry Moore sculpture that they kept under glass, Ethan told me. He went to Cornell, too. I liked how Ethan seemed so obviously connected to his family; the affection he conveyed for his siblings reminded me of my own, a complicated kind of devotion. After a few glasses of the Chianti del Cuore, or whatever it was we were drinking, I was able to loosen the tight grip I was keeping on my silverware and napkin and give him the rundown on my family. My oldest sister, Nancy, a psychology professor living in Orange County, is divorced and has one daughter I don't see as often as I'd like. The next is Carla, a yoga instructor and voice teacher; she is married to Ken, and they have a son named Max. Neither of my brothers was married at the time; Nick was living in Japan (he brought his wife, Yuki, home from there), and Matthew was a reporter for a newspaper in Connecticut (where he later met his wife, Elizabeth). Ethan listened intently enough, and when the check came, I let him pick it up, even though he hesitated. The restaurant gifted me with a ceramic heart-shaped box wrapped in red cellophane, which made Ethan crack a smile and further exacerbated my discomfiture, though I held on to that piece of kitsch for years and years.

Ethan tried to end the date when our walk home took him to his block. I was not ready to release him.

"You can't go home now, it's only eleven o'clock. Come over for a bourbon and soda," I implored.

Ethan refused at first but eventually agreed after I insisted.

Back at my apartment, I mixed our drinks. Ethan had never had bourbon with soda and lime (my drink of choice at the moment) and complimented the concoction. I figured that might keep him in my audience a while longer. To further that goal, I ricocheted back and forth from the sofa to the CD player, trying to impress him with the greatest hits from my collection while wondering if my butt looked big in my gray-and-brown plaid Chaiken pants as I stood in front of my stereo changing disks. I hadn't dressed up too much for the date, wanting to seem casual, but there was nothing casual about my intentions. I wanted confirmation that Ethan liked me. I wanted to kiss Ethan. I was getting nowhere. Ethan remained burrowed in his corner of the sofa.

"What does it take to seduce you?" I finally blurted out, foggy with alcohol and anxiety.

Ethan's face erupted into a nervous smile that would become all too familiar. "I think we should just be friends."

What does it take *to seduce you?*

How was I all of a sudden channeling *Dynasty*'s Alexis Carrington? I never even watched that show. The words haunted me as I slept, lightly, that night. I awoke hung over and full of dread.

"It was all going fine until I threw myself at him!" I exclaimed to Ginia, and later to Anne on the phone. (I couldn't admit what I had actually said.) The next evening I was sitting with Jen, recalling the horror for the umpteenth time, when the phone rang. It was Ethan.

"I had fun on our date," he said. "We should do it again."

What?!

Between that call and the next from Ethan, I got involved with a sexy fuck-up who graduated from Columbia University but whose present occupation was drawing pictures of fish for a company that made T-shirts sold at resort areas like Paradise Island or Antigua. I never cooked for him; we mostly hung around his East Village apartment and sang songs while he accompanied on guitar. The Rolling Stones' "Dead Flowers" was the one he kept returning to.

"Send me dead flowers to my wedding," it goes, "and I won't forget to put roses on your grave." Eric didn't hide the fact that he was still in love with his ex-girlfriend Evgenia. No doubt he was thinking about her when he sang that song, but I sang along anyway. On less rueful nights, we lay in bed singing every television commercial jingle we could remember. Eric was a bit of a sad sack, but he was soulful and bore the sharp edge of a depressed, underachieving Ivy League graduate. I tried to lure him to Brooklyn with the promise of a home-cooked meal—God knows he needed one—but he canceled at the last minute, griping about a cold-sore outbreak.

Ethan got in touch again, and we made a plan to watch the Oscars at my place. Though I was caught up with Eric and his dead flowers, I still thought enough of Ethan to offer to make dinner. I consulted with Anne on what to make, and she suggested something healthy, indicating that Ethan liked his food clean. I came up with this pasta mixed with cancer-fighting vegetables and antioxidant fruit and nuts: penne, with a sauce of broccoli, sautéed in garlic, sprinkled with plump raisins and toasted walnuts.

~~~ ~~ ~~ ~~ ~~

Healthy Penne

- 1 pound broccoli (or 1 nice bunch)
- 2 tablespoons olive oil, plus a little more for finishing
- 1 clove garlic, chopped
- Pinch hot red pepper flakes
- 1/2 cup raisins
- Salt
- 1/2 cup chopped walnuts
- 1/2 pound penne
- Freshly grated parmigiano cheese

Wash the broccoli and cut into florets; discard the stalks. In a skillet large enough to hold the pasta and broccoli, heat the olive oil over medium heat, then add garlic and red pepper. When the garlic is golden, add the broccoli, raisins, and a big pinch of salt. Sauté for 15 to 20 minutes, adding a little water if the mixture gets too dry. Meanwhile, toast the walnuts in a small skillet for 5 to 6 minutes over medium heat, giving the skillet a shake every so often. Watch them or they will burn! Once they are toasted, remove from heat and set aside.

Cook the pasta according to the directions on page 32. Drain and add the penne to the skillet with the broccoli, then add a splash of olive oil and the toasted walnuts.

Serve in warm bowls. Pass the parmigiano at the table. (If you are lactose intolerant—Ethan was, but somehow cheese didn't bother him—you may substitute 1/4 cup toasted bread crumbs for the cheese and it is equally scrumptious.) Feel more or less virtuous that you had vegetables with your carbs.

Serves 2, with leftovers.

Titanic won nearly every award, but, unlike Kate Winslet, I did not get a kiss at the end of the evening. All Ethan asked for was a doggie bag.

I do not consider myself a woman who gets the things she desperately wants, and God may have good reasons for this. Nor am I foolish enough to pursue what is undoubtedly impossible. But Ethan gave just enough to keep my hopes up. Calls and e-mails arrived with regularity. Returning from Saturday brunch with my girlfriends, I'd be shocked to find a phone message from him asking what I was up to. Electronically we'd bat notes back and forth, debating the relative merits of John Lennon's versus Paul McCartney's post-Beatles solo work. I loved Wings, Ethan preferred Lennon, but he did like McCartney's pre-Wings stuff, so he made me a tape of Paul's first two solo albums and wrote each song's title on the sleeve, a romantic gesture if ever there was one. Meanwhile, Eric dumped me, declaring definitively that he was still in love with Evgenia. I bought my first pair of Gucci shoes and promptly stopped wondering why Eric couldn't love me and started wondering if charging $457 to my credit card was really such a good idea.

Ethan wouldn't go away. When summer came, he managed to appear at our Shelter Island house every weekend, even though he hadn't bought a share. When I analyzed this habit, I was forced to admit there could have been other reasons besides me that he might do this. It's an island, and an incredibly relaxing one at that. You have to take a ferry to get there, and the voyage gives you the sense of leaving everything behind. Our house, a converted eighteenth-century rectory, was as magical as the island. It had a pool in front and a trellis of wisteria in back, beneath which we ate lunch al fresco. The house was owned by a family of artists whose paintings covered the walls. The furniture was cozy and the kitchen well equipped. The dining room table accommodated as many

as twelve. Usually we were eight staying in the house, and we often invited
over other friends from the island or
the Hamptons for carefully planned and
beautifully executed dinners.

We would arrive on Fridays and barely
leave the compound except to grocery
shop; we got the tastiest tomatoes, eggplants, squash, and basil from a stand attended by no one, where the prices were
written on a chalkboard and you slipped
money through a slot in a red padlocked
box. We bought our fish from the Com-
mander, a retired navy man whose shop,
in the basement of his house, sold fish
fresh and fried, though mostly the Com-
mander just seemed to be getting baked.
The house was full of excellent cooks,
chief among them Anne, who would hang
back and take a managerial role most of
the time, then wow us with some imaginative treat like lavender ice cream. Another new friend, Astrid, would whip up
Spanish tortillas, cold borscht, or won-
derfully marinated flank steak. Her boy-

friend, Robert, an academic from Poland, was the naked mascot of the summerhouse; he liked to delve into everyone's personal lives and gave good advice administered poolside as he sunbathed in the nude. Belinda and Jeremy, a journalist and architect from Australia, were not cooks, though the one confection they contributed—barbecued bananas sliced down the middle with chocolate melted inside—was one of the most memorable desserts in a summer chock-full of them. Most nights we got so carried away with talking and drinking wine that we didn't get dinner on the table before ten o'clock.

The first thing I ever made for Ethan on Shelter Island was a Sicilian recipe that originated with my grandmother: halibut baked with a sweet-and-sour sauce of red wine vinegar, yellow onions, raisins, and mint. I was overcome by Ethan's admiration for this dish, which I interpreted as thinly veiled praise of me. He was still raving about it by the pool the next day.

～～ ～～ ～～ ～～

Unforgettable Halibut

1/4 cup olive oil

6 yellow onions, sliced 1/4 inch thick

2 teaspoons salt, plus extra salt to taste

1/4 cup red wine vinegar

2 tablespoons honey

1/4 cup currants

1 cup fresh mint, chopped

3 pounds halibut, or 6 (8-ounce) portions of
   any firm white fish—cod, sea bass, snapper,
   or flounder will work well, too

Olive oil for brushing

Freshly ground pepper

Preheat oven to 450 degrees.

Heat the olive oil in a large sauté pan over medium-high heat. Add the onions and sprinkle with 1 teaspoon salt. Cook onions, stirring occasionally, until they are soft, 15 to 20 minutes. Add the vinegar and honey and cook for 5 minutes. Then add the currants and 1/2 cup of the chopped mint, cook for a few more minutes, and taste for salt (add more if necessary).

Brush the halibut and baking dish with olive oil, sprinkle fish with 1 teaspoon salt, and cover with the onions. Bake for 15 to 20 minutes depending on thickness of the fish.

Remove to serving plate and sprinkle with freshly ground pepper and remaining mint.

Serves 6.

I didn't have to urge Ethan to come out to the house with me early on Friday afternoons, he always suggested it. I was able to get a jump on dinner thanks to publishing's traditional summer hours. Ethan, being a writer, was free to accompany me, and accompany me he did. He'd join me on my shopping rounds, hang out in the kitchen while I prepped and cooked, then sit with me on the couch and drink wine while we waited for the others to arrive. Conversation never lacked for a moment, whether I was trying to convince him to like me (which I couldn't help doing after a glass or two of wine) or my favorite band, Pulp. The latter he could not abide, and as for the former, well, he never managed to come up with a convincing argument for either side of the issue.

Ethan had warmed up to me enough that a hand or other limb of his would find its way to some unthreatening part of my body whenever we were sitting together. Once, not entirely as the result of my own movements, I found myself so close to him that a kiss was practically unavoidable. Ethan didn't fight me off, nor did he respond with much passion. Then the phone rang and it was time to collect our friends at the ferry. Alone in the house again the following Friday, I tried to pick up where we'd left off while waiting for a pot of water to boil for linguine that I would dress with a sauce of shrimps, scallops, and white wine. That old smile of Ethan's returned as he reiterated his friendly intentions toward me. I was saved from whatever hopeless explanation he was about to offer by the eruption of bubbles bursting through the lid of the stockpot.

"As much as I care about you, what concerns me most is getting dinner ready," I warbled as I fled to the kitchen, taking on a cloak of false cheerfulness as I attended to:

~~~~~~~~~~~~

Linguine with Friendly Little Fish
(Adapted from Jennifer Romanello)

   2 tablespoons olive oil, plus extra for taste
   1 clove garlic, minced
   Pinch hot red pepper flakes
   1/2 pound shrimp (buy them already cleaned, if
      available, and remove tails)
   1/2 pound scallops, sea or bay (if sea, cut into
      quarters)
   1/2 cup dry white wine
   1 pound linguine
   1/2 cup chopped parsley

This is a quick and easy sauce that can be made while the pasta is cooking; you don't want to cook the fish too long or it will dry out.

In a medium sauté pan, heat the olive oil and then add the garlic and red pepper. Sauté for 2 to 3 minutes until golden, then add the fish and white wine. Cook until shrimp are pink and scallops are solid white.

Meanwhile, cook linguine according to the directions on page 32. Drain well and add to the fish, stirring gently. Add a splash of olive oil and the chopped parsley, then divide into warmed bowls. You *do not* serve fish pasta with cheese. (My mother does, but it's a bad habit.)

Serves 4 as a main course, 6 as a first.

Minor disappointments and crushing blows abounded, yet Ethan and I did grow close that summer. In addition to eating, we were both into biking, for which the conditions on Shelter Island are ideal. Together we explored every corner of that island, riding for hours while gabbing about our eternally amusing housemates and their precarious relationships. Midway through the summer, Robert dropped Astrid for a younger woman he met in Poland. She looked like a model, but she had all the energy of a dying swan. He was back with Astrid by summer's end; no amount of beauty and youth could compare with that woman's cooking. And what was up with Stacey's boyfriend, Hank? He'd arrive at the house with a rolling suitcase full of work and yet was involved in no projects as far as we knew. Stacey's father had similar questions about his authenticity and had gotten a private investigator on the case, Ethan told me. Ethan was concerned for his friend, but he wanted to like Hank. I did, too, especially since Hank's desire to get Ethan and me together rivaled my own. He acted as our couples counselor, trying harder than I ever did to extract information from Ethan about his reluctance to get involved. He'd grill him at dinner, over drinks on the porch, during swims in the lake, on jogs, and on walks. I seconded his every inquiry.

"What will we do when summer's over?" Ethan asked when we dismounted at Shell Beach, a jetty that sticks out half a mile into the bay, where we always took a break from our weekly ride. I didn't know why he was so concerned, since we were just friends and all, but I wanted to help.

"I'll invite you to dinner parties," I replied, hoping I could win him in the cooler months with my talent as a hostess. On the way back we'd pass Crescent Beach, which faces west, just as the sun was setting. Our housemates wondered what we were up to on those long rides. I wondered why the long rides were all we were up to.

When the fall came we went on double dates with Stacey and Hank, though only one of the couples was dating. One evening over margaritas in TriBeCa, Hank got to grilling Ethan about us and wouldn't let up. I sat there thoroughly amused. Ethan, usually so reticent, wasn't uncomfortable; in fact, he seemed to be enjoying the attention as much as I was. Hank convinced him to go home with me that night. When we arrived at my apartment, we found my brother Nick there; he was in town with no place to stay, so he had let himself in for the night. It was impossible to explain what Ethan and I were in the middle of, though it was far more innocent than whatever my older brother must have conjured. No, we weren't there for a night of wild passion, we were enrolled in a remedial dating course, and we were going to give simple kissing a go.

"We can go to my place," Ethan said, but I wanted to be on my turf, so I quickly dispatched Nick to his friend Al's apartment in Sheepshead Bay.

When we were alone, Ethan made the truly grand admission that he had discussed me with his therapist, but he didn't tell me what he said. Evidently, Ethan was struggling with his feelings for me; I just couldn't understand why it was such a struggle. We did kiss, though, with Stevie Wonder's *Fulfillingness' First Finale* playing in the background. "There're brighter days ahead," went the first song. We kissed through the entire album, and when it was done Ethan went home.

Our relationship continued to focus on music. Ethan invited me to come and sing with his band. I had never really sung in front of anyone except along to the radio or CDs in the car, and here I was supposed to belt one out in front of Ethan's friends, whom I had just met. A bottle of Budweiser from the six-pack we picked up beforehand helped relieve the tension, and my performance improved as the evening wore on. I took the mike and delivered brash statements with great timidity. I sang Madonna's "Burning Up" (incredibly appropriate) and

AC/DC's "You Shook Me All Night Long" (less so). Ethan's agility with the opening guitar line of the Beatles' "And Your Bird Can Sing," an incredibly complicated riff, was pretty hot. When we got tired of playing, we'd repair to some nearby pub for hamburgers and more beer. It was a successful enough pairing that we repeated the experience many times, always beginning with a beer and moving through our repertoire of rock and pop classics. The band seemed like a constructive solution to all my unrequited feelings. I had given up on there being anything more between us.

But that may be because I somehow intuited that Ethan was about to come around.

"You look nice for your date," he told me in the elevator to the practice room. I had informed him that I wouldn't be making it to our regular postmusic burgers that evening, and I could tell from Ethan's voice that he wasn't exactly thrilled about my assignation. Nor should I have been: Daniel Eisenberg, the guy I had been seeing, was to dump me over dinner that night, using a Liz Phair line to explain himself. "I'm a complicated communicator," he told me. I wished he had simply communicated on the phone his wish to not see me anymore so I could have hung out with my band mates, rather than dragging me out for a meal I couldn't enjoy eating while he explained to me the ways in which we "didn't click."

I took that one way harder than I needed to, since Daniel and I had been out only a few times. But the combination of that marginal disappointment in the shadow of the Ethan situation just made me feel hopeless. Here was a man I had everything in common with, a man in whose company I was most at ease and happy and who gave me no indication that he felt any differently, and yet he wouldn't or couldn't be with me for some mysterious reason.

It was laughable, really. And so I laughed myself into a day off from work

and an extra therapy session. I laugh-
ingly made Ginia come over for breakfast
to console me on Saturday morning, and
then, with laughter, I accepted my lot.
Love just wasn't going to happen for me.
I decided I was fine with it. It was Hal-
loween. I put on the costume of acqui-
escence; my four-year-old nephew, Max,
dressed as a Hoover vacuum cleaner. We
went trick-or-treating, and then I called
Ethan to confirm plans for later that evening. We were going together to a dinner
party.

"Helloooo, pumpkin!" I chirped when
I called him. The greeting was authentic.
I didn't resent him, this was my life; it
was okay. Before dinner, I met him at his
apartment. I had never visited him there
before. Interestingly, on top of the stereo
was a pile of brand-new Stevie Wonder
CDs. Could this have had anything to do
with the fact that I had played him Stevie
Wonder the last time he'd come over? He
hadn't confessed to liking him before. He
threw them in his five-CD changer and

hit the shuffle button. He explained that that was his way of taking in new music. I liked the idea, but I wouldn't be able to execute it, working, at the time, with just a Sony Discman hooked up to components I'd had since high school.

It was looking more and more like something was up with Ethan when he followed me to a party after dinner. It was already eleven-thirty, and he usually liked to be tucked in by midnight. We ended up sitting on the radiator in front of the window, talking to no one but each other, telling our stories of "the first time." After that, Ethan, who usually just dropped me off on the corner, walked me to my door. There he spoke the most romantic words a man has ever said to a woman: "Can I come up to your apartment? I have to pee." He lived only a few blocks away; that's when I knew for sure that Ethan was looking for more than just the use of my porcelain.

We spent half an hour looking at a book of Yiddish expressions I kept on the coffee table, a gift from my author Henry, who knew I was a Yiddish enthusiast. Ethan especially liked all the ones having to do with the *tuches.* I had to reach past the book to kiss him, but he did not resist. After we kissed for a song or two (*Fulfillingness' First Finale* again, brighter days, increasingly imminent), Ethan stopped and held me for a very long time. His surrender was palpable. Even when we got into my bed together, I wasn't convinced anything would happen, and now even I wasn't inclined to force it. I put on a nightgown, albeit a conservatively sexy one. It didn't stay on.

"Unprecedented," is how Ethan labeled what took place over the next four hours. I later looked up the word to try to extract further meaning from it. I did that with the word *auspicious,* too. That's the one he assigned to Drovers Tap Room, which was where we met.

Those words were bandied about over a breakfast of pumpkin-walnut bread that I happened to have left over from the consolation call Ginia had paid the previous morning when I was mourning the complicated communicator. How everything had changed in just twenty-four hours!

~~~ ~~~ ~~~ ~~~

Morning After Pumpkin Bread

(Adapted from Vern Bertagna, *Bon Appétit*)

- 1/2 cup (1 stick) butter, softened
- 1 1/2 cups sugar
- 2 large eggs
- 1 cup canned pumpkin
- 1 1/2 cups self-rising flour
- 1/2 teaspoon ground cloves
- 1/2 teaspoon ground cinnamon
- 1/2 teaspoon ground ginger
- 1/2 cup walnuts, chopped

Preheat oven to 350 degrees.

Butter and flour a 9-inch loaf pan. Beat butter and sugar with an electric mixer on medium speed until blended, then add eggs and pumpkin. Sift flour with the spices in another bowl, add to pumpkin mixture, mix in walnuts, and pour batter into buttered pan.

Bake until tester inserted into the middle comes out clean, about 1 hour and 10 minutes. Transfer to a cooling rack and cool in pan for 10 minutes, then release the edges with a knife and turn onto rack to cool completely.

Yield: 6 to 8 servings.

Of course, a night together didn't necessarily mean Ethan was mine. But the nine-month lead-up indicated this was not a man ruled by whims. The stirring display I witnessed on Saturday night betrayed some strong feelings on Ethan's part. Still, as dreamy as I felt about what had occurred, I didn't allow myself to be swept away by fantasies. But when Ethan called on Tuesday to see what I was up to that evening, I could think of only one thing: I wanted to make him dinner.

I made a tangy risotto with Taleggio

cheese and artichoke hearts. Much like love, risotto requires a lot of work and patience. That was all behind me with Ethan, at least for the moment, and I was ready to put in some vigorous stirs for old times' sake.

~~~~~~~~~~

Risotto with Intricately Layered Hearts

> **4 cups hot chicken broth**
>
> **2 tablespoons unsalted butter**
>
> **1/2 small onion, minced**
>
> **1 cup arborio or carnaroli rice**
>
> **1/4 cup white wine**
>
> **1 cup canned artichoke hearts, chopped**
>
> **1/2 cup Taleggio, cubed**
>
> **Salt to taste**
>
> **Freshly ground pepper**

Keep the chicken broth on the stove over medium heat.

In a large sauté pan or Dutch oven, melt 1 tablespoon butter over medium heat and add the onion. Cook until onion is transparent, about 2 minutes, then add the rice and toast it with the butter and onion until the grains are translucent, about 2 minutes. Add the wine, stirring constantly until the wine is absorbed, then begin to add the hot chicken broth a ladleful at a time, stirring until the liquid is absorbed into the rice.

Continue adding the stock and stirring the risotto until it is creamy and the grains are softened but not mushy. Begin to taste the risotto after about 15 minutes to check the texture, but more likely it will take 20 to 25 minutes of stirring vigilance. (Heck, you waited nine months for Ethan, what's another half hour?) If you run out of stock and the risotto needs more cooking, use water warmed in the pot with the stock.

When you are happy with the texture of the rice, remove it from the heat, add the remaining tablespoon of butter, the artichoke hearts, and the Taleggio, give it one more stir, test for salt, let it sit for a minute, and serve with freshly ground pepper.

Yield: 2 servings.

I was so excited that this relationship I had craved so long was finally mine that for the first few weeks I could barely sleep when Ethan was in my bed. I would spring up early in the morning, go straight to the kitchen, and start putting away the dishes from the previous night. Squeezing all the pots and pans into one cupboard made quite a racket. I apologized for the noise.

"Actually, I find it comforting," he told me.

Ethan loved everything having to do with food and being cared for. Which worked out well, because once we were together I was overcome by a drive to cook beyond anything I had ever known before. I was jealous of Anne over all the amazing meals she must have made for him.

I was haunted by thoughts of them the way other women might be troubled by visions of complex acrobatics their boyfriend performed in bed with previous girlfriends. Not that I didn't worry about that, too. But still, cooking was mine. It relaxed me. It had become, next to Ethan, the most important thing. It was a way to make sense out of my internal chaos. There is logic and order to cooking. What you put into it has everything to do with what you get out of it. With love, it's not so cut-and-dried.

Ethan and I talked a lot about what we were going to eat. While a phone call asking about dinner had been grating to Kit, for Ethan it was a welcome break from writing. We stayed on the phone and disputed the pros and cons of various dishes for many hours, all paid for by my employer. Sometimes we'd decide to go out, but more frequently I turned to the computer, called up epicurious.com, and sought out recipes to suit Ethan's mood. This salmon with lemon-tarragon butter became a simple everyday meal for us, though it's impressive enough, when presented on a bed of lentils, to be served to guests.

~~~~~~~~~~~~~

Tuesday Night Dinner

These recipes serve 2 but can be doubled.

Salmon with Lemon-Tarragon Butter

(Adapted from epicurious.com)

> **3 tablespoons unsalted butter**
> **Juice and zest of 1 large lemon**
> **Freshly ground pepper**
> **2 salmon fillets**
> **Salt**
> **1 1/2 tablespoons fresh tarragon, minced**

In a small saucepan over low heat, melt butter with lemon juice and zest, remove from heat.

Place salmon skin side down on a broiler pan. Brush with half the butter mixture, season with salt and peper. Broil until just cooked through, about 20 minutes (there is no need to turn).

Transfer to plates. (Salmon skin will stick to the broiler pan. I always think I should save it to make sushi from this delicacy, but I never do.) Add tarragon to remaining lemon butter. Spoon over salmon and serve over lentils.

Serves 2.

~~~ ~~~ ~~~ ~~~

French Lentil Stew

(Adapted from Nigella Lawson, *The New York Times*)

1 shallot
1 clove garlic
1/2 stalk celery
1/2 carrot, peeled
2 tablespoons olive oil
1 cup French lentils
1/2 teaspoon dried thyme
1 bay leaf
1 1/2 teaspoons salt

Finely chop the shallot, garlic, celery, and carrot. It's easiest to do them all together in a food processor if you have one. Heat the olive oil in a sauté pan over medium heat. When the oil is hot, add the vegetables and cook until they have softened (about 5 minutes), then add 3 cups of water, lentils, thyme, bay leaf, and salt. Bring to a steady simmer, then lower heat. Allow the lentils to cook for 20 to 25 minutes. When they are tender and have absorbed most of the water, they are ready to serve; if they are still a little tough, add more water and continue to cook until softened.

Serves 2.

Baby Arugula and Avocado Salad

(Adapted from Levana Kirschenbaum)

2 cups baby arugula

1 small head endive

1/2 avocado

1 1/2 tablespoons olive oil

1 1/2 teaspoons unfiltered apple cider vinegar

1/2 teaspoon sea salt

Freshly ground pepper

Wash and dry arugula. Slice the endive crosswise into 1/4-inch strips. Cut the avocado into 1/2-inch-wide pieces. Toss the above in a large bowl with the oil and vinegar, then add salt and a few grindings of black pepper.

Serves 2.

Ethan complimented the dinners I made in e-mails sealed with a kiss (SWAK, they'd say in the manner of fourth-grade girls signing one another's autograph books; I loved that). He was as enthusiastic about me as he was about my food. In person he'd compliment my face, saying I had a "cute *punim*." He was a more affectionate boyfriend than I would have ever dreamed he'd be, and what's more, he was more than I ever imagined a boyfriend could be. He was the holy grail of boyfriends, a companion of the opposite sex who was as much fun and as easy to be with as a girlfriend—even better than a girlfriend because we got to have sex, too. Which I have never been inclined to do with a girlfriend, no matter how much I adore all of mine and even though I went to Sarah Lawrence, where everyone tells you you eventually will.

There was no person in the world that I felt happier with than Ethan. He was the most important person in my life; he came before my friends, he came before my family. He drew me in and away into our own little world. I welcomed the separation. We had food, we had music, and in bed we had pleasure and laughter in equal measure. Most of all, we had misanthropy. We made up nasty little scenarios and songs about our relatives and acquaintances, none of which I can share. Trust me, they were hilarious, even if Ethan and I were the only ones who could understand just how funny they were.

I will never laugh as hard as I did the night I made us too much soup. It was a cold winter Sunday, and I had just purchased a twelve-quart stockpot. I filled it with chicken and vegetables and herbs and finished it off with noodles and tiny meatballs. But it was just Ethan and me and those twelve quarts. Being my father's daughter, I was a little concerned about waste, so I ate three bowls to Ethan's two. We were having so much fun at the table that when the phone rang, I didn't bother to get up to answer it. Later that evening, I checked the message. It was from Ethan's friend David, a Manhattanite who happened to be in the neighborhood with his girlfriend and wanted to stop by. I cursed myself for not picking up the phone. They could have had some soup!

Later, in bed, Ethan teased me about my fixation over this. We joked that he could take the stockpot, strap it onto a dolly with bungee cords, and share it with the guys at his MTV writers' meeting the next day. As he ladled it out to them, he would enact a law that all of their girlfriends had to sign up for soup duty. "So, Rick, can I put your Ilene down for a potato leek?" he said in the voice of an old man from Brooklyn. The thought of Ilene Rosenzweig, a newspaper editor and design entrepreneur, who does have a domestic side but was in no way the *balabusta* I was, making soup for the writers' meeting had me laughing so hard that I was gasping for breath as tears were pouring out of my eyes. I kept waking up through the night in hysterics thinking of that line. Ethan awoke to find me doubled over and clutching my stomach; then he started laughing, too.

Ethan rarely left my side, even when it wasn't dinnertime. When I got a bike, he bought the male twin of mine. He went to my hairdresser, Randall. We'd make back-to-back appointments—Ethan got his cut while I sat, with foils on my head, waiting for my highlights to take. "If you're willing to let him see that, it must be love," Randall pronounced. Even people who didn't know us thought we made a perfect pair; when we ran into Henry having lunch with one of his exes, he later told me that she pointed us out to him, saying, "That's a happy couple."

I brought Ethan along with me to book parties and dinners with authors, where he tuned in to career dissatisfaction I wasn't ready to face. "You're hiding your light under a bushel," he would say. I agreed, but I didn't want to think about it. Instead, I sublimated my creative inclinations into making meals for Ethan. I didn't want any more, or at least that's what I told myself; I just wanted to be his wife. He could be the artistic one while quietly admiring all the madcap things about me, like that "What does it take to seduce you?" line, which, one evening, he confessed to finding the most adorable thing he had ever heard.

Ethan even got a kick out of my mother's nonsensical expressions, like "What's new in the world of sports?" her typical greeting for him, and "Here's to us, long may we wave," her toast at every meal. It's clear where I got my gift for strange turns of phrase. Because Ethan could appreciate and even contribute to the madness, he fit right in. I couldn't help but find Ethan's rich uncle—whose wife sent us to the supermarket every time we visited their Hamptons estate with an enormous shopping list that seemed to include the family's grocery needs for the entire summer (everything from ketchup to toilet bowl cleaner to lightbulbs), then gave Ethan a hard time when he asked for reimbursement—somewhat ridiculous. But behind our lighthearted disdain for those we were stuck with from birth was a whole pantry of love and loyalty. Because Ethan was so devoted to his family, I wanted to become part of it and for him to become part of mine.

Which meant getting on planes, lots of them. I went to Detroit, Tucson, and Des Moines. All places I had never visited before that I was perfectly content to see. Ethan was the first boyfriend whose family I ever met. I never went to North Dakota to meet Kit's mother, which always worried my own, enough for her to gently prod every now and then, "Why haven't you met his mother?" Here in marked contrast, I was thrilled that Ethan cared enough to introduce me to his sisters, cousins, nieces, and nephews. We saw many more members of his family than we did mine—we don't really have a lot in common with our American first cousins, we have some second and third cousins in Pittsburgh we see every now and then, and a lot of cousins we are crazy about in Italy (most likely because they are in Italy). On those trips with Ethan's family, I frequently ended up doing the cooking whenever his uncle, the *macher,* wasn't taking us out. Word got around that I was competent in the kitchen, and while at first I jumped at the chance to impress his parents with improvised risotto primavera or impromptu beef bourguignon, I eventually got annoyed when everyone looked to me to take charge of every meal.

Ethan's mother, like me, had been a woman with a firm belief in the importance of cooking to please your man. Sadly, by the time I met her, she was suffering from dementia, which struck her at an unfairly early age. But, wanting to get to know the mother of the man I loved, I spent a good deal of time with her alone on those visits. We took long walks together and even managed to make each other laugh with harsh critiques of the neighbor's gardens. Ethan and his dad would hang back at the house, watching the French Open or *Carnal Knowledge* on TV, the latter of which I found somewhat disturbing when I walked in on the last few moments.

Ethan, wanting to show me the person his mother was in her prime, shared a copy of her favorite cookbook, *Thoughts for Buffets*. In the margins she had written notes about her husband's reaction to each dish: "Allen liked!" they said, or, "Less salt next time!" I chuckled at her simple prefeminist housewife inclinations, but I had no reason to. I was cut from the very same cloth.

When we got home from our first trip together, to Iowa for his sister's fortieth birthday, I asked Ethan if he loved me.

He replied in the affirmative without any dithering. From then on, he would tell me he loved me unprompted. Still, I don't know if it was me, or the fact that it took so long to win him, or the one night a week he insisted on spending at his own apartment, but somehow I never stopped feeling that I was one meal away from Ethan's love. I like to joke that I went to the Ethan Binder School of Cooking, because in my inexhaustible drive to please him, I ran myself into the ground pulling off gastronomic feats I might not otherwise have tried.

At Passover I made Ethan a seder, taking two days off from work to prepare the many traditional dishes from scratch. This one nearly broke me. Done in after the first day of cooking, I got testy with Ethan. "Your religion hates women!" I barked when I greeted him at the door that evening.

Ethan, who didn't do well with confrontation, got defensive: "I didn't ask you to do it!" It's true, he hadn't, but I had to get angry at someone. Being familiar with the Old Testament, I knew it was best not to take it out on Yahweh. Ethan rebounded well from my wrath, showing up with roses in hand when it came time for the actual event.

I rolled matzo balls and dropped them in the homemade chicken broth that had simmered all day on the stove; chopped apples into tiny slivers and toasted and ground walnuts for the *haroseth;* grated fresh horseradish by hand to sprinkle on top. I used Ethan's mother's brisket recipe, which, like my previous boyfriend's mother's recipe, contained onion soup mix as well as chili sauce. That's what I made, and it was perfectly fine, but I'm going to spare you the Lipton and Heinz and provide instead this wonderful sweet-and-sour brisket (which does include Coca-Cola) from Levana Kirschenbaum, Jen Warren's kosher cooking guru. Sometimes I go with Jen to her classes. Levana prides herself on the simplicity of her recipes. "If this is difficult, then nothing is easy," she says. She's a witty and engaging teacher, and even this shiksa picks up a handy hint or two when I'm there—like how to make preserved lemons (put them in a jar with salt and store them for three weeks). Unable to avoid throwing in a bit of my own culture, I made broccoli di rape—it's not an herb, but it can be bitter when not prepared correctly.

~~~~~~~~~~~~~

A Seder for Nonbelievers

Levana Kirschenbaum's Sweet-and-Sour Brisket

   1 medium onion, peeled and quartered
   1 (2-inch) piece ginger, peeled
   6 large garlic cloves, peeled
   1/2 cup Dijon mustard
   1/2 cup red wine
   1/2 cup Coca-Cola
   1/2 cup ketchup
   1/4 cup honey
   1/4 cup cider vinegar
   1/4 cup soy sauce

1/2 cup olive oil
1 teaspoon ground cloves
1 tablespoon coarsely ground pepper
1 (6- to 7-pound) first-cut brisket

Preheat oven to 350 degrees.

Combine onion, ginger, garlic, and mustard in a food processor until smooth. Add the remaining marinade ingredients and process a few more seconds.

Place the brisket in a pan just large enough to fit the meat, then pour the marinade over it, cover tightly with foil, and bake for 2 hours. After 2 hours, turn the brisket and bake uncovered for 1 more hour.

Remove brisket to a cutting board and tent with foil. Strain pan liquids into a small saucepan over medium heat and reduce to about 2 cups. When the brisket has cooled slightly, slice it thin and pour gravy over it. Pass additional gravy at the table.

Yield: 8 to 10 servings.

~~~ ~~~ ~~~ ~~~

Broccoli di Rape

2 pounds broccoli di rape (or broccoli rabe or whatever your vegetable purveyor calls it)
Salt
2 tablespoons olive oil
2 cloves garlic, minced
1/8 teaspoon hot red pepper flakes

Place a large pot of water over high heat. Arrange a large bowl with water and ice. Trim the tough stalks from the broccoli, and when the water begins to simmer, add salt and then the broccoli. Blanch for 3 minutes (to remove some of the bitterness), then drain and place in the ice bath.

Heat the olive oil in a large skillet over medium heat, then add the garlic and hot pepper. When the garlic is golden, drain the broccoli, squeeze out the excess water, and add it to the skillet. Lower the heat and cook for about 10 minutes for crunchy broccoli, 20 minutes for soft;

add a little water to the pan if it gets too dry.

Serves 6.

~~~ ~~~ ~~~ ~~~

Chicken Soup

The components of a good chicken soup are very flexible, and variations of this recipe will probably work out fine.

2 to 3 pounds any combination of chicken
    parts, or 1 whole chicken, even the gizzards
1 medium white onion, peeled and cut in half
2 celery stalks (if they have leaves, keep them)
2 carrots, peeled and cut in half
1 parsnip, peeled and quartered
1/4 cup parsley
1/4 cup dill
2 tablespoons salt
Dill for garnish

Place all ingredients in an 8-quart stock-pot, add about 3 quarts of water (enough to cover and then some), turn the heat to medium-high, and bring to a boil.

When the water is boiling, use a strainer to skim the foam that rises to the top. Keep the soup at a slow simmer and cook for 1 hour.

Strain all the solids; you can use the chicken for chicken salad, or you can remove the fat, cut the meat into little pieces, and serve in the soup with the matzo balls if you are in the mood for something heartier. Garnish each bowl with a little dill snipped with scissors.

You could make this same soup and, instead of matzo balls, drop in the meatballs from page 186. No need to brown them; let them cook in the broth and do the same with 1 cup of egg noodles 10 minutes before serving.

Yield: 8 to 10 servings.

~~~~~~~~~~~

Matzo Balls

4 eggs
4 tablespoons light olive oil
4 tablespoons cold seltzer

1 teaspoon salt
1/4 teaspoon white pepper
1 cup matzo meal
Salt for water
Dill for garnish

In a medium bowl, whisk together the eggs and oil, add the seltzer, salt, and pepper, then gradually whisk in the matzo meal and continue whisking until thoroughly blended. Cover with plastic wrap and refrigerate for 15 to 30 minutes.

Bring a large pot of salted water to boil. When the mixture is chilled, roll into balls, using 1 heaping tablespoon for each matzo ball, as they will expand during cooking. Drop them into the water. Lower the heat and bring the water to a simmer, then cover and cook for 45 minutes.

Remove the cooked matzo balls from the water and add them to the chicken soup. Serve garnished with some dill snipped with scissors.

Yield: 14 to 16 servings.

"This is the first seder that's really my own," Ethan said as he presided over the Haggadah reading. That text, from Exodus, got him thinking. "I just don't like this motif that the Jews think they're chosen," he said. The statement was right in line with Ethan's lack of faith in himself. How could he believe in the idea of being a member of a race chosen by God when he had absolutely no grasp of his own potential? As successful as he was, Ethan could have been even more so. His trajectory was littered with episodes of opportunity knocking and Ethan staying away from the door. When he aspired to be a musician, he sent a demo tape to Alan McGee, the legendary British producer who discovered Oasis. McGee actually called Ethan, but Ethan never returned the call. If you don't know McGee, let's just say this is up there with wanting to be an animated dinosaur and ignoring a text from Steven Spielberg. Jann Wenner, legendary editor and founder of *Rolling Stone*, liked the few profiles Ethan had written for the magazine and wanted to offer him a contract. Instead he decided to leave magazines and get into television, which granted may have been a better place for him, but what I'm trying to say is that Ethan took no joy in his accomplishments. Stacey, who was rediscovering her faith, took issue with his reading, as did Hank (who was in the midst of converting). Me, I was just happy to hear I made Ethan a seder he thought of as his own.

We went to Rome for our first trip together, where I introduced him to my favorite restaurants and took him to some of the better shops, like Ermenegildo Zegna and J. P. Tod's. Ethan's style—which included an appalling leather jacket with some kind of weird belt attachment before I got my hands on him—received some badly needed improvement under my watch, though I'm afraid I created a bit of a monster on that front. Ethan spent hours in those stores trying to decide between the blue shirt or the beige or whether to get the shoes in a forty-four or forty-five— neither ever felt right. He pushed my nerves to the limit when we missed a hard-won lunch reservation at Il Moro because we spent too much time at a boutique where the salesclerk took enormous interest in outfitting him from head to toe. "I couldn't help it. He dressed me up like a little doll!" said Ethan, who bought almost everything he tried on, including the shoes, which eventually proved to be uncomfortable and remained unworn when they repatriated to the United States.

His reaction to the shoes was no stunner. Comfort was paramount to Ethan—the elusive thing he was constantly searching for but couldn't find. It was what I desperately wanted to give him, if I could only figure out a way to do it. "You don't know me!" he'd shout in the voice of an angry old curmudgeon whenever I'd try to suggest something I thought might be good for him, like insoles or shoe trees. No one slept as poorly as he did, no one's back or neck hurt as much as his. He was alone in his creaky body.

I brushed cod in butter like Ben-Gay and wrapped it in prosciutto—just the way Ethan dressed his neck on a particularly stressful visit to his parents' home in Tucson.

〜〜 〜〜 〜〜 〜〜

Orthopedic Cod

(Adapted from Nigella Lawson, *The New York Times*)

It won't make Ethan's neck feel any better, but it is delicious.

> **2 (6- to 8-ounce) cod fillets**
> **3 tablespoons butter, melted**
> **4 slices prosciutto**
> **1 heaping tablespoon chopped parsley**

Preheat oven to 400 degrees.

Brush the cod fillets with half the melted butter; wrap each piece in two slices of prosciutto, then brush again with the remaining butter. Place on a baking sheet lined with foil and bake for 20 minutes.

Serve immediately over lentils from page 81, with parsley sprinkled on top.

Yield: 2 servings.

He did find some approximation of comfort on the artichoke-hued "shabby chic" sofa I purchased the very day we met. It was big and soft and enveloping, not to mention a perfect vantage point from which to watch dinner being made. On winter Sunday afternoons, as the sun was going down, Ethan and I would lie there side by side and listen to music. Early on, he had convinced me to buy a five-CD changer just like his own and had helped me lug it home and build a new set of shelves to house it. The sofa was the one thing I had that was just right. He liked it so much that he wanted to get a similar one for himself. This became the weekend activity for a good part of our relationship. Saturday and Sunday afternoons would find us at Macy's, Crate & Barrel, Pottery Barn, or Bloomingdale's looking for a couch as cozy as mine for Ethan to buy for his own apartment. When he found one that seemed like a possibility, he would conduct a number of tests. First he'd sit on it; if it proved to be acceptable for this basic utility, he would lie down on it to confirm that it was of a suitable length. How the arms cradled his head was a crucial factor for maximum reading and television-viewing pleasure. If the prospective sofa passed all those tests, I would be beckoned to lie down next to him to see how well we fit on it together. I went along with this exercise, feigning complicity, but I didn't like what it represented. I pictured our lives merging, along with our furniture; Ethan was working on a "separate but equal" scenario. I spent a lot of time on my therapist's couch talking about Ethan's sofa shopping.

I worried, too, whenever he asked me how to make one of his favorite dishes. What would he need me for if he had my sofa and my recipe for tomato sauce? But Ethan never bought a sofa, and he never learned to cook, at least not while he was with me.

———

I came so far with my own cooking while I was with Ethan that I began to prefer it to going out for meals 99 percent of the time. Dining in restaurants is disappointing more often than not, I have learned. Even in the most celebrated restaurants— *especially* in the most celebrated restaurants. It's impossible for anything to live up to expectations set so high. There's chemistry involved in making a magical night out. Where you are sitting, your mood and that of your date, your rapport with the server, all these elements are as important as the food, and rarely do they all combine in harmony. Still, when you hit it, it's so superb that it's worth taking the chance and going out every so often. In any case, even this cook needs a break every once in a while.

Asian food is one cuisine worth leaving the house for because it's sensational, and as much as I love to cook, you are never going to find me rolling up raw fish in rice and seaweed or doing much with fish sauce or sesame oil. I stick to Western themes in my cooking. Ethan's favorite food, besides anything that I made, was sushi. Back in the late nineties when we were dating, Nobu was *the* place for Japanese food, but if you weren't Robert De Niro or Heidi Klum, good luck getting a table at dinner. I had been there for lunch on my expense account a couple of times and always wanted to take Ethan because I knew he would love it. One evening when we weren't getting anywhere with one of our what-to-have-for-dinner conversations, we got it into our heads to try our luck there. Ethan and I walked in with no reservation, approached the model-look-alike maître d' at the podium, and boldly asked if there was a table available. She hesitated a moment, looked into her computer, and announced a sudden cancellation.

We ordered the omakase—a multi-course meal of dishes chosen by the chef—and a bottle of crisp sauvignon blanc. As each delicacy arrived before us—black miso cod or a piece of the freshest toro—Ethan was overcome with emotions emitted in fits of uncontrollable laughter. I didn't know whether to be concerned or pleased (I *was* buying). I ended up feeling a little jealous of those fish: I was never treated to an outburst akin to the one the uni at Nobu received. I hoped that Ethan's feelings for me were as deep as the sea our dinner came from, but I wasn't convinced.

Ethan was with me for the present, but I wasn't so clear about our future. I wanted us to be married, but conversations on that subject, which I began to broach after about a year, were not encouraging. I first confronted him on a day when I learned of fabulous successes from two of my best friends. Ginia had just been hired by *The New York Times,* and Jen Warren had gotten engaged. I, on the other hand, was still working in a publicity job that I could do with my hands tied behind my back and dating a guy with a record of long relationships that never made it to the chuppah. That evening Ethan and I went to dinner at Saul, our favorite local restaurant, where, by no fault of its own, a few of our heavy semi-conversations ended up taking place. As soon as the busboy poured our water, I blurted out that question which . . . well, if you have to ask it, you already know the answer:

"What are you thinking about us?"

"I'm not thinking anything," Ethan said.

Disturbed, and unable to achieve satisfaction from whatever follow-up questions I composed in an effort to ascertain some idea of our prospects, I ended up weeping into the bread basket while Ethan worried about what the waiter would think.

We went to Venice for Ethan's fortieth birthday. In the preceding weeks, I mapped out all the restaurants we would go to and made reservations. Over fritto misto at the legendary Da Fiore, I decided to give the subject of marriage another go.

"Now that you're turning forty, don't you think it's time to get married?" I asked, sounding like his mother or a concerned aunt. Ethan looked at me as if I had suggested that this milestone might be a good time to consider a move to Equatorial Guinea.

I spent much of that weekend despondent as we wound our way through the canals in the rain. I cried or sulked through most of the meals, however delicious.

"What makes you so sure we *won't* get married?" Ethan asked me as I wept in the customs line at Malpensa Airport after crying for four hours straight on the train from Venice to Milan. Ever impenetrable, Ethan gave me no signal as to what he was going through, if he was in conflict over a decision or if he wasn't "thinking anything." All I know is that I hate Venice.

I decided to lay off the subject for a few months.

———

On New Year's Eve, we opted for a quiet dinner at home. I found a recipe for a salad with mâche, a tiny, nutty leaf Ethan favored. After a long day of food shopping with no break for lunch, I finally got to the vegetable market; because they carried a pretty sophisticated selection of greens, it never occurred to me they wouldn't have what I was looking for.

"If you had called me earlier in the week, I could have ordered it for you," the proprietor told me.

I wanted to kick myself. How could I have neglected to call ahead for a rare green that was essential to my menu? I tried another store, and another, but nobody had mâche. I considered getting on the subway and heading to Manhattan, where I certainly would have found it, but I didn't have the energy to go that far. Famished and bushed, I settled for some boring Boston lettuce torn into tiny pieces. Ethan didn't know the difference, but I was miserable the entire evening. My dinner wasn't perfect, and I wanted every dinner to be perfect, especially this one.

~~~~~~~~~~~

A Salad That Failed to Make a Perfect New Year's Eve

Mâche, Pomegranate, and Pecan Salad

(Adapted from *Gourmet* magazine)

- 1 pomegranate
- 1/2 teaspoon sugar
- 1/2 teaspoon red wine vinegar
- 1 tablespoon extra-virgin olive oil
- 1 cup mâche (widely available these days, to my chagrin)
- 2 tablespoons chopped pecans, toasted
- Salt and pepper to taste

Cut the pomegranate in half crosswise and remove seeds from one half; juice the other with a citrus juicer or reamer as you would an orange. In a small saucepan, simmer juice, sugar, and vinegar until it reduces to about 1 tablespoon, then cool

to room temperature. Divide dressing between two salad plates and drizzle with
oil. Divide mâche, pecans, and reserved
seeds between plates and season with
salt and pepper.

Serves 2.

In the end, no quantity of mâche was
going to make Ethan Binder marry me.
After three years I decided it was hopeless. I took a final stand by delivering my
ultimatum: I refused to go on the next
Binder family expedition—a trip to Detroit to celebrate Ethan's father's seven-
tieth birthday, which fell on the same
day as my thirty-fifth birthday—unless
we were engaged. Surely that would do
it—his family loved me, and he had a
much better time with them when I was
around.

Ethan went without me.

Mitch Smith Licked the Plate

Our first date was blind for me but not for him. Mitch had seen me before at Henry's book party three years earlier when I had just started dating Ethan. He liked the fact that I was looking all over the place, taking everything in, he later told me. If that was indeed my mission at this party, I failed, as I hadn't even noticed him. I hadn't a clue whom Henry was referring to when he called me the next day to say that his friend Mitch had a crush on me.

"Are things still working out with you and Shiny?" asked Henry, using a nickname he'd created for Ethan because he thought he had a shiny forehead. (Ethan

despised the moniker—and, for that reason and others, Henry himself.) I told
Henry they were. Still, I was curious.

"Who is he?" I asked.

"He's a writer, he had two novels published; the first one was made into a
movie."

I wanted to know more, even after hearing the movie went straight to video.

"I don't know him that well. I see
him at book parties, sometimes we
play basketball together, he goes to AA
meetings," said Henry, blithely violating
the eponymous principle of Alcoholics
Anonymous.

So Mitch was in recovery with Henry.
That didn't bother me. Alcoholism in the
background adds complexity—maybe
even complications; I like those. Having
lived with and loved an alcoholic in denial,
I admire anyone who has recognized and
faced his problem. Kit went through too
much before he finally did.

A quick peek at Amazon revealed that I
could find Mitch's books a few yards from

where I was sitting. They were published by Simon & Schuster, my employer at the time. I went down the hall to the book room where old backlist titles were stored and scanned the shelves, found a copy of his first novel, and took it to my office. I closed the door. I checked out the author photo and read the flap copy. The novel was about a fifteen-year-old girl who really wants to have sex with some guy in a band. Mitch was kind of a punk rock Judy Blume. I felt a twinge of remorse about missing out on him.

I spent a summer mourning for Ethan. When it was over, I thought of Mitch. I called Henry.

"Hey, remember that guy you told me about who liked me at your book party three years ago?" I said to him on the phone.

"Mitch Smith, yeah."

"Do you think he'd want to go out with me now?" I asked.

"Let me find out."

Mitch called the next day.

"Good old Henry," Mitch said, his voice sounding craggy and vaguely Irish on the phone.

We agreed to meet the following Tuesday for coffee at a place not far from my office, the Coffee Pot. He chose it. Because of his sobriety, Mitch did most of his dating in coffee bars; he seemed to know every café in Manhattan and most of the ones in Brooklyn. Mitch worked at home, writing in his Williamsburg apartment, a Brooklyn neighborhood not easily accessible to my own.

This was just after September 11, 2001. In those weeks, I did as the president advised: I bought stuff. Work was quiet, since most author tours and publicity had been canceled. The novel I was pushing about a madcap graphic design professor at a state college in western Pennsylvania in the early 1980s could by no means be reinterpreted to fit the moment. Bored at my desk, I regularly snuck out of the office in the middle of the day and wandered the stores of Rockefeller Center, checking out the plentiful sale racks, buying outfits, doing my part to stimulate the economy. I also succumbed to the lure of cable television, after priding myself on being one of the last holdouts. Without the signal cast from the top of the World Trade Center, there was no more free television in Brooklyn. Those were strange and lonely days. You needed TV. Even more than that, I needed a new boyfriend. *The Sopranos* could effectively distract me from the world's problems, but it was going to take more than Carmela's incorrect but terribly familiar pronunciation of "sfogliatelle," my favorite Neopolitan pastry, to help me get over Ethan.

I was buoyed by the promise of this mystery man who already liked me. In the days between that phone call and our date, I went for long runs and thought about him. I didn't have much to go on besides some racy prose of his that came up in a Google search, but it was enough to get my blood going as I took the final hill of Prospect Park's 5K loop. When Tuesday finally came, I put my body— superslim from grief and exercise—into a new knee-length, kick-pleat khaki skirt from H&M, a clingy low-cut black sweater from Banana Republic, and burgundy kitten-heel sling-backs from Saks and made my way over to the Coffee Pot in the cool late October twilight. Though I had only a hazy memory of Mitch's author photo, I intuited that he was the guy least resembling a person waiting for his date to arrive. He was sitting far from the entrance, staring into the screen of the café's sole computer. I boldly walked up to him and found I had guessed right. Somehow, maybe from the bits I had read on the Internet, I could just tell this one was going to be tricky. Up close, Mitch appeared harmless. His hair was gray-flecked brown and very short; he wore horn-rimmed glasses, a burgundy Le Tigre shirt, jeans, and Adidas sneakers. He dressed younger than his years, but the look suited him. He carried the clothes of a twenty-something on his forty-something body with elegant ease.

"I just came back from my baby brother's wedding," was one of the first things Mitch said to me, waving a folded five-dollar bill in the air to indicate that our drinks were on him as we waited in line for coffee. I was a bit taken aback that he would mention a wedding so soon into our semiblind date. *The Rules,* my ill-begotten dating bible, instructs women never to utter the word *wedding* or *marriage* in any context whatsoever on a first date. I didn't appreciate the double standard. The wedding took place in Portland, Oregon, where Mitch grew up and where his parents still lived. The baby brother was well into his thirties.

We took our coffee over to a high table in the middle of the room and sat across from each other on stools. Mitch talked about his writing career; he even happened to have with him some photocopies of reviews from his first and second novels, which I pretended to read. After our date he was going to stop by the post office to mail them to an agent he was pursuing. *Oh, Lord, another insecure writer,* the practical hemisphere of my brain warned, *I have enough of those in my work life.* But the more powerful hemisphere, the one containing the desperate-to-be-loved-by-impossible-men matter, found this writer cute and curiously captivating. As we talked, I didn't get the sense that Mitch and I were connecting, though things got a little more intimate when we moved on to the subject of psychotherapy. I was disappointed to learn that he had recently quit seeing a low-cost shrink-in-training at New York University Hospital. Any help is good help, I thought, and though I'd known Mitch for only a few minutes, it was clear he needed some. After all, who doesn't? But Mitch didn't think the treatment was getting him anywhere; he was going to try Buddhist meditation instead. I prefer Western solutions to mental unease, even if I wasn't totally sold on my own psychologist. I had been seeing the same man I began "working with" right before I started dating Ethan. The therapist, like most of my boyfriends, seemed more interested in my recipes than in "my issues." The subject of food came up often; that was my doing. But did I really need his advice on adding orange rind to cranberry sauce when we were talking about Thanksgiving dinner? Sure, that's a good tip, but when it came to handy hints about how to get over Ethan—the reason I was seeing him—he had no cherished recipes to pass along. My help would have to come from other sources. I was relying on Mitch, even if love seemed like a long shot during the coffee portion of our date because he was talking a lot and I was talking a little and the points of intersection, as far as dialogue was concerned, seemed few and far between. Things got better when he walked me to the subway.

"You have beautiful eyes," Mitch said apropos of nothing as we made our way down Ninth Avenue. Now we were getting somewhere. It had taken two hours, but finally I'd received indication of some attraction on Mitch's part. Knowing that he liked me at that party so long ago—enough to call me three years later—had added extra pressure to the evening. Up till now, I wondered if he was disappointed with me. Whether I was disappointed in him was not a matter I gave a second's thought; I needed to be loved again, and soon.

As we continued walking, Mitch confessed that he had Googled me before our date. He found an old review of a Pulp concert I wrote for *Addicted to Noise,* a now defunct online music magazine my brother Matthew edited and that everyone in the family (except my mother) and more than a few of our friends wrote for at some point. The review was a billet-doux to Jarvis Cocker, Pulp's front man at the time, of whom I am a devoted fan. Mitch joked that he considered getting some tinted glasses, Jarvis's signature accessory, to wear on our date. I didn't admit that I had Googled Mitch, too.

"What CD do you have in your CD player right now?" I asked as we walked through Bryant Park. Someone once asked me this question on a first date; I thought it made for a good game. You could get caught with something embarrassing like Olivia Newton-John, if you happened to be in such a mood that day—and if you were honest. Mitch told me he was listening to the Strokes, a New York band that everyone in the world would know in about a week. I made a mental note to get their CD the next day. When we got to Fifth Avenue, Mitch stopped and kissed me on the mouth.

"You wanna go see a movie on Saturday night?" he asked as we looped around the block to the subway.

"Sure," I said.

Then he grabbed my hand and pulled me over to an iron grate near the subway entrance, where we kissed some more.

"Your glasses are fogging up," I said

to Mitch when we stopped to take a breath.

"Of course they are."

I was excited and famished when I got down to the subway. It was nine o'clock, and I had not eaten since lunch. My hunger only made me more wired; my head spun as I tried to process my thoughts about this quirky new man and, of course, what I was going to make myself for dinner. I decided on something simple made from things I already had on my shelves: farfalle with tuna, white wine, capers, and onions. I needed a sturdy dish to bring me back to earth.

~~~ ~~~ ~~~

First-Date Butterflies

Salt

2 cups (about 4 ounces) farfalle

1 tablespoon olive oil

1/2 medium onion, chopped

Pinch red hot pepper flakes

1 (6-ounce) can tuna packed in olive oil
   (essential!): Progresso or any brand imported

**from Italy will do nicely, but I even use
Bumble Bee's version, and it's fine!**
1 tablespoon capers
1/4 teaspoon salt
3 tablespoons dry white wine
Splash olive oil
2 tablespoons chopped Italian parsley
Freshly ground pepper

Bring a large pot of water to boil over high heat. This sauce is so quick and easy, you can make it while the pasta is cooking. When the water is boiling rapidly, add a large dose of salt and the pasta, then cover the pot until the water is boiling rapidly again. Uncover the pot and give it a few good stirs.

Meanwhile, heat the olive oil in a medium skillet over medium heat, add the onion and hot pepper, and sauté until translucent, about 2 minutes. Open the can of tuna and drain as much of the oil as possible (I do this by pressing the disengaged top of the can against the tuna over the sink with as much force as I can muster). Add the tuna to the onions, then the capers, the salt, and the wine. Lower heat and cook until the pasta is ready.

Drain the pasta and add it to the skillet with the tuna, add a splash of olive oil, the chopped parsley, and a few grindings of black pepper.

Serves 2, or 1, with enough for lunch the next day.

I ate the pasta while watching a telethon to raise money for families of 9/11 victims. The theme of this one was a John Lennon tribute. Sean Lennon performed, and Yoko, too. When Kevin Spacey took the stage to do a pretty impressive cover of "Mind Games," it felt way too appropriate. I couldn't wait a minute longer to call Ginia and tell her about how it went with Mitch.

There is no one like Ginia to ratchet up my excitement about a date. She indulges in flights of fancy I wouldn't dare entertain, which is precisely why I always call her first. By the end of the conversation, she is sure to have me as good as married, with two kids, a steadily growing college fund, and money saved for retirement. This can get me worked up in ways that are detrimental to my better judgment, but tonight I needed the fantasy, and Ginia was there, as always, to provide it. She was happy for me, especially in light of the fact that she'd had a front-row seat to all my sadness that summer.

We had rented a house on Shelter Island for August, which I wasn't inclined to do because of all the memories of Ethan there, but Ginia convinced me to do it, and it turned out to be the right thing. She, too, was single at the time. We borrowed my brother Matthew's old white Volkswagen Beetle, a convertible with leopard-skin seat covers, to drive around the island—where we couldn't get enough of looking at rich people's houses and imagining the gracious living going on behind the gorgeous facades— and take to parties in the Hamptons. In between long conversations on the front porch about what in the world Ethan could be thinking and what he might be doing, which always concluded with the revelation that he wasn't good enough for me anyway, usually followed by a crying jag, we managed to enjoy the summer.

I needed all the help in the universe to cope with my despair; I even called upon God. On Sunday mornings, I rode my lonely twin Raleigh (now divorced from its partner at Ethan's) to Our Lady of the Isle Roman Catholic Church on Shelter Island. I cried during most of the Mass. Sometimes I sang along to songs I remembered from my Catholic school days, led by a geriatric choir accompanied by a Hammond organ. I felt a little hope when I noticed a couple of attractive men who regularly attended Mass alone. The one who wore a madras blazer and drove a Mercedes convertible from the early seventies had to be gay, but another, whom I often ended up sitting next to, probably wasn't. He had an English

accent and drove a silver BMW convertible. How lovely that he maintained his
faith, and the Catholic one at that. So exotic for a Brit! During Paul's Second Letter to the Thessalonians, I filled out his
story in my head. He was a banker sent
over to the New York office of a British
firm, Barclays, perhaps. While the choir
plodded through a particularly flat ren-
dition of "Were You There When They
Crucified My Lord?" I fantasized about
approaching this man, whom Ginia and
I had come to call "Nigel," and inviting
him to our house for dinner. But I never
mustered the courage to speak to him,
apart from saying, "Peace be with you,"
when it came to that part of the Mass, so
I was free to focus all my dating anxieties on Mitch.

I figured he would call the day after
our date, but he waited until the day after
that. By then, the Saturday night movie
he'd suggested had been traded for an
excursion to Williamsburg with a bunch
of his friends to see a band.

"Sounds fun," I lied.

"Okay, I'll call you Saturday afternoon to shore up plans," said Mitch.

I was disappointed, not only because I was looking forward to being alone with Mitch, but also because this meant I would have to come up with Williamsburg-appropriate attire. Williamsburg, the hipster capital of New York City, if not the entire world, was not my scene, even if I might be attracted to the sort of man who lived there. I spent all of Saturday morning shopping for an outfit while waiting for the "shore up" call on my cell phone. The call finally came; the outfit did not. (One doesn't shop in Boerum Hill boutiques for Williamsburg date wear, I was to learn; one goes to the Salvation Army.) I became more optimistic about our date when Mitch said he would swing by my place to pick me up so we could have dinner in my neighborhood. I pulled a Tocca dress from a few seasons back (home-grown vintage!) from my closet: a scoop-necked, cap-sleeved, purple wool tweed minidress. I wore it with brown leather high-heeled boots.

I was glad that Mitch would see my apartment. I was fond of the place where I had, at that point, been living for ten years; I believed it revealed likable things about me. The records, for instance: There on chrome shelves—assembled by Ethan to replace a hand-painted leaning tower I rather liked but he believed to be dangerous—sat every one I ever purchased dating back to 1978, a collection of more than two hundred, including a twelve-inch extended dance mix of Men Without Hats' "The Safety Dance," which, come to think of it, could have been tossed a few years earlier. I imagined inviting Mitch to "come up and see my vinyl" when he arrived at the door. I'm always looking for witty openers for awkward encounters like therapy appointments or second dates.

When the blaring doorbell signaled Mitch's arrival, my heart pounded as I tried to make my way slowly to the door.

When I opened it, I greeted him with a peck on the lips. I did not use the vinyl comment, thank God. But the kiss wasn't such a great idea, either. Mitch seemed distant and uncomfortable. He came in and nestled into a corner of the couch. I offered him one of the nonalcoholic beverages I had purchased while on my fruitless search for a dress. I brought two Cokes over to the sofa and sat opposite him. It wasn't long before, without my even having to bring up Kurt Cobain, or Hole, or drug abuse, or even the city of Seattle, he mentioned that he had once been friends with Courtney Love.

"Did you sleep with her?" I asked.

Mitch was coy, though bringing up the subject was plainly designed to elicit that very question. I was inexplicably intrigued.

I took Mitch down Smith Street, the now revitalized Brooklyn boulevard that had transformed—despite Ethan's nega-tive pronouncement during that Valen-tine's Day date three years earlier—from a desolate stretch of bodegas and old-lady underwear stores into an impressive row of restaurants and boutiques. While I tried to figure out where we should eat, Mitch talked about some band he had seen on Conan O'Brien called At the Drive-In that was destined to be the hottest thing. Mitch didn't strike me as the fine dining type, and I had no idea what he could afford among the pricey options. In lieu of the Polish or Greek diner I assumed Mitch was accustomed to, I settled on a simple Italian café, Paninoteca; they specialized in pressed sandwiches of melted cheeses and cured hams. I could have a much needed glass of wine, and it wouldn't be too expensive.

I was fond of my neighborhood, I even considered it hip, but walking through it with Mitch gave me the impression that what registered as hip to me did not for him. Mitch was posthip. "Emo" was the thing, he explained as he ate a salad, though he wasn't so good at defining what seemed to be a philosophy that covered both music and fashion. After a twenty-minute conversation, all I knew was that it had something to do with looking, or acting, or sounding, like a librarian. Was that all it took to turn on Mitch Smith? I could certainly opt for my glasses, instead of my usual contact lenses, for our next date—if there was one.

I felt decidedly square as Mitch rattled on about the many different cities—Los Angeles, San Francisco, Portland, and Prague—he had lived in over the past few years. Since 1991 I had lived in the same apartment, the one I'd moved into with Kit. Before he got sober, Mitch took a lot of drugs and slept with strung-out punk girls. My brief dalliance with illegal substances never led me down any road more perilous than the consumption of too many Hostess CupCakes. I slept with Jewish boys who had back problems. Mitch didn't ask me many questions, and when he did, they were the wrong ones. Like "Were you a lesbian in college?" I didn't have the requisite alternative answer to that.

The check totaled $21.95.

"Do you want some money?" I asked.

"If you want to," Mitch replied.

I didn't want to. Giving him that ten was humiliating, but I duly handed it over.

Back on Smith Street we ran into Henry, who was amazed to see us out together.

"I can't believe neither of you e-mailed me! How long have you been hanging out? Is this the first time?" he said.

"Actually, we're engaged," said Mitch.

Mitch's sense of humor was mostly hidden until that moment. Instead he seemed intent on impressing me, or more likely alienating me, with a litany of references designed to prove how cool he was. Not unlike a character from a novel written for teenagers, only here there was no older, wiser person to advise him to just "be yourself."

We took the G train—a mysterious line that stopped at Bergen Street, my regular subway stop, but I never had any occasion to use—to Williamsburg. The G is the only line in the entire New York City transit system that does not go to Manhattan. This underdog train took on a new sense of purpose as Williamsburg and its environs became a living destination for young hipsters. It snakes through Brooklyn to Long Island City, which is actually in Queens. I marveled at the stops as we passed them: Fulton Street, Clinton-Washington Avenues, Classon Avenue. Where in God's name were we? But the question that was really burning through my mind was: Why was I feeling so awful?

"Are you okay?" Mitch asked, noticing my discomfort. He took my hand and then, perhaps thinking that wasn't the cool thing to do, quickly withdrew it. Instead he soothed me by mocking himself: "You know you're on a hot date with Mitch when it's eleven o'clock and you're riding the G train," he pronounced, and I laughed.

We exited at Metropolitan Avenue—which I'd seen hundreds of times from the vantage point of a car on the Brooklyn-Queens Expressway—and walked over to Pete's Candy Store. The place was cute, like its name, with a bar up in the front, a middle room where bands play, and a garden, which was where Mitch's friends were assembled with pitchers of beer. I drank some; Mitch had a Coke. We talked to them for a little while and then went to the other room to watch the band. Mitch put his arm around me as we listened, then he gave me one of those little cheek kisses, as he had done on the street the previous Tuesday. It was two in the morning when we left.

When we got to the subway, Mitch pointed me in the direction of the westbound platform and explained that the eastbound train was the one that took him home.

"You're not going to make me take

the G alone at two in the morning," I protested.

"How stupid of me, of course I can't do that. I'm such a terrible date," Mitch exclaimed.

"There are several areas in need of improvement," I replied.

I wanted Mitch to come home with me not only because I was concerned for my safety, but also because I was still hoping I could turn this date, and the way I felt about Mitch, and the way Mitch made me feel about myself, into something more akin to our previous date.

"Well, since you came all the way here, you may as well come up and watch some TV," I said, pretending not to care whether he did or not, when we arrived at my door. We lay on the couch side by side, watching videos on MTV. Things got cozy, and soon enough we were making out. This was when I discovered where Mitch really shines on a date. It was incredibly exciting to kiss him and be touched by him, even though when he reached into my dress he couldn't re-sist criticizing it.

"What is this itchy material?" he asked.

We didn't go far, but there was some-thing about fooling around with Mitch that I really, really liked. It was altogether unlike sitting across from him at a res-taurant or beside him on a train. Here we were in synch while he introduced compelling story lines that were left un-completed when he finally said: "Thanks for a fun evening." We kissed for a little while longer by the door, then he said, "See ya," and descended the front stoop.

See ya.

What did that mean? Would I in fact be seeing him again? I couldn't hazard a guess. The next morning, I met Jen and her husband, Jeff, at Barney Greengrass for brunch and a fruitless analysis of the date and the possible meanings of the phrase *see ya* over bagels and whitefish

salad. Jeff always likes to help me dis-
sect dates and is usually quite astute, but
even he couldn't make heads or tails of
this one, and of course neither of them
could understand why I cared so much,
anyway. Monday after work I went running, then stayed home and waited for
Mitch to call. Tuesday I went to a benefit at the American Museum of Natural
History and made believe I was someone
who wasn't waiting for a call. Wednesday at 9:48 in the evening, the phone
rang. Mitch and I talked for a while and
covered topics that were, to my relief, a
little more bourgeois. Turned out Mitch's
father was a doctor, too: an orthopedic
surgeon.

"Do you play tennis?" he asked.

"A little, why?"

"I have a theory that all the children of
doctors know how to play tennis."

Now we were on the same court, as it
were—a couple of normal middle-class kids
with round-robin in their backgrounds.
Mitch had shed the pose of social deviance

he was affecting four days earlier. I was cheered by our smooth interaction, ready to laugh off the Saturday disaster as simply an aberration. We were both nervous, I thought, we'll go on another date and it will be fun again like our first.

"Well, call me if you know of any parties," Mitch said before hanging up.

I didn't. I also didn't know what to do next, so I read his first novel, the one about the girl who wants to have sex with the guy in the band. When I finished I sent him an e-mail saying that I loved the book. I really did. Judy Blume is still one of my favorite authors and I love music, so the combination of the two appealed to me. And I am acquainted with enough writers to know that none lives who can ignore a compliment of their work.

Mitch called me the next afternoon, and I, in a last-ditch power grab, didn't call back. Monday morning he e-mailed and asked me if I wanted to go to a movie that Saturday night.

"Yes," I wrote back.

"Okay. But you'll have to pay for your-self," he replied.

This was supposed to be a joke. It wasn't funny; I did pay for myself—and Mitch paid for himself with a ten-dollar bill, all the better to ensure that no one—not me, not the ticket clerk, not the guy behind us—would mistake him for someone who might be buying two tickets.

After *Riding in Cars with Boys*, a movie about teenage sex, Mitch came over and we had approaching-middle-age sex. It was as I thought it would be. Mitch, for all of his dopey hipster pos-turing, was incredibly sexy. I became instantly hooked on being with him and hoped we could develop something out of bed that more closely resembled what went on in it.

And much as he resisted, I could tell that Mitch was getting attached, too. "I can't believe I slept over," he said the next day. "But when I woke up and saw the sun and trees out your windows, I knew I was in the right place." Naturally, I wasn't in the bed when he woke up. I was in the kitchen making coffee and putting together a batter for pancakes. I added a touch of vanilla, which Mitch disapproved of. He liked his pancakes "without flavor." Who tastes vanilla? I wondered. It just enhances. Mitch could. The vanilla was the pea under his pile of mattresses.

～～～～～～～～

Unflavored Pancakes

(Adapted from Mark Bittman, *The New York Times*)

I would add 1 teaspoon of vanilla or a little orange zest, and you should, too, but not if you're dating Mitch Smith.

> **1 cup flour**
> **1 tablespoon sugar**
> **1 teaspoon baking powder**
> **1 egg**
> **1 cup milk**
> **Butter**

Mix the first five ingredients until just combined. You don't want to overwork the batter; Mitch is enough trouble as it is.

Heat a nonstick griddle over medium-high heat and melt 1 teaspoon butter per round of pancakes. When the butter is sizzling, drop 1/4 cup batter for each 5-inch-diameter pancake. Cook until dry bubbles form (about 1 minute), then cook the other side for about 30 seconds.

Yield: 8 pancakes.

Our intense physical attraction made those early dates feel special, even with Mitch's occasional grievances. Still, I could never be sure if I'd hear from him again each time we parted. But I was determined to get something in particular from his erratic presence in my life, a desire I fulfilled when I ran into Ethan at the gym one Saturday morning a few weeks into my thing with Mitch. I stopped to talk to him as he pedaled a stationary bike, white, gym-provided towel around his neck, *New Yorker* magazine balanced on the handlebars. I abandoned my exercise to talk to him, and since we couldn't stop talking (this hadn't changed even after the breakup), we decided to finish our workouts and then meet for lunch. While stretching, I concocted a sly way of letting him know I was seeing someone.

Knowing the topic of music would come up (it's either that or restaurants in the postdating version of Ethan and Giulia), I would tell him I was into the Strokes and find a way to let him know who turned me on to them.

"Who are you rocking out to these days?" I asked as we sat across from each other at one of the Smith Street bistros even he was embracing.

Badly Drawn Boy, a less than rocking singer-songwriter I hadn't yet heard, was Ethan's pick.

"Who told you about them?" I asked, hoping that he'd ask the same question when I told him about the Strokes.

He did.

"Some guy," I replied with a false breeziness that needed no interpretation. Ethan didn't take it well. He accused me of trying to humiliate him; I retaliated by blaming him for putting me into the position of wanting to humiliate him.

"My despair is bottomless," I said, ever the Sarah Bernhardt in his presence.

I took way too much pleasure in the knowledge that it killed Ethan to know I was with another guy, especially one with such good taste in music. Clearly I wasn't quite over him, so I threw renewed effort into worrying about Mitch, who was, as usual, taking the maximum time allowed by ancient codes to get back in touch.

I heard from him next on election day, and when I chided him for taking so long to call, he told me he wasn't interested in a relationship, he wanted to be "friends."

Distraught on the F train on my way back to Brooklyn, I came up with this:

"If we're friends, why can't we have sex?"

I tried it out on Mitch when I called him from outside my polling place on my cell phone. The line was stolen directly from his first novel, which could be why it worked.

"I'll come over," Mitch said.

I voted, then went home and whipped up a pear cake to serve him with post-coital coffee.

~~~ ~~ ~~ ~~~

Pear Cake for Friends with Benefits

(Adapted from *Bon Appétit* magazine)

   2 large eggs
   1/2 cup butter, melted and cooled slightly
   1/4 cup whole milk
   2/3 cup plus 1 tablespoon sugar
   1 1/2 cups self-rising flour
   4 Bartlett pears, peeled, quartered, cored, and cut crosswise into 1/4-inch-thick slices
   Confectioners' sugar

Preheat oven to 375° degrees.

Butter and flour an 8-inch cake pan. Whisk eggs, melted butter, and milk in a large bowl. Whisk in 2/3 cup sugar. Add flour and whisk until batter is smooth. Mix in pears. Transfer batter to pan and sprinkle top with remaining 1 tablespoon sugar. Bake until top is golden and tester inserted into center comes out clean, about 40 minutes.

Cool in pan, then invert onto a plate and sprinkle confectioners' sugar on top. This cake is wonderful made with summer peaches, too.

Yield: 8 servings.

We didn't even say hello. We just started kissing the second Mitch walked in the door. His glasses fell to the floor and got a little bent; his iPod, whose earphones were still in his ears for the first few seconds, also hit the ground and took some scratches. It was like a scene from a teen version of *9½ Weeks*. We did it on the couch with the Strokes playing in the background.

Afterward I made coffee, and Mitch dropped cake crumbs all over his chest and my sofa as he tried to eat a rather large slice while lying beside me. I didn't mind; I was happy watching election returns with Mitch, and the cake was pretty awesome, too (to use a Mitch word). Mike Bloomberg became mayor, and Mitch stayed over. But we were *not* dating!

While I waited for my friend's next call, I wondered if alcohol might have had anything to do with the slow approach in getting to know Mitch. I had never been with a guy who didn't drink. I craved those relaxed, bonding moments that bloom easily over a shared bottle of wine. We weren't going to have any of those. Mitch was committed to his sobriety, which was certainly impor-tant for him but wasn't doing a whole heck of a lot for me. How could anyone possibly fall in love without grown-up refreshments?

The next week, Mitch invited me to go bowling with "some publishing people." I like bowling about as much as I enjoy getting my teeth cleaned, but I wanted to see Mitch, so I went and put on the disgusting shoes and bowled and even got a strike or two. The friends were more impressive than I expected friends of Mitch to be. There was an editor from the *Paris Review,* a literary scout, an independent film producer. They drank pitchers of beer, but I stuck with Coca-Cola in solidarity with my sober "friend."

"What's going on with us?" I asked Mitch later that evening when we were by ourselves, eating French fries at Corner Bistro. "We have these amazing times together, then I don't hear from you for six or seven days. I can't go on like this."

"I'm afraid of you," Mitch said.

"You're hurting my feelings," I told him.

Apparently, Mitch didn't know I had any. I tried to convince him I did (if you can imagine such a conversation, and you will have to, as I have permanently blocked it out of my mind) and that he had some sway over them. I think he heard me a little. We got somewhere that night, somewhere a couple of martinis (gin, please) could have gotten us to a lot faster. Out on Waverly Place, we made a date for the weekend. Before I jumped into a cab, Mitch slipped a piece of Bazooka bubble gum into the pocket of my denim jacket, where it stayed for five years. Each time I wore that jacket and felt the gum in there, it reminded me of the first time I felt connected to Mitch outside of bed.

Food wasn't really Mitch's thing, not the way it was with Ethan, but he expressed extraordinary fondness for everything I ever made for him. And I didn't have to work very hard at all; even a simple spaghetti with butter (cook spaghetti until it's al dente, swirl around a little unsalted butter, add a heaping tablespoon of parmigiano cheese, grind some coarse pepper on top), which is what I made for him that Saturday as a late night snack, sent him right over the moon. Mitch liked it so much that he licked the plate. He tried to hide this from me by ducking behind my shoulder to do it as we sat on the couch, watching TV while we ate, but I caught him and was probably meant to. He thought this was the most amusing anecdote in the world, a confirmation of his belief that he was a mere hayseed with no knowledge of how to behave in my commanding presence.

He accompanied me to church the next morning and held my hand during the service. The weekend after that, I went to Miami for a book fair. I ran on the beach every day, thinking about Mitch and listening to the Strokes on my iPod. While I was there, he sent a postcard to my house. It said something about missing me, or so he says; I never received it. He said it was the most romantic thing he had ever done.

From then on, Mitch stayed over at my apartment nearly every night. This was never planned. Inevitably at around nine o'clock I'd get a call from an unknown number; it would be Mitch calling from the cell of some other AA member (he went to meetings just about every evening, and he didn't have his own phone). I'd be done with whatever drink or dinner thing I had that evening with another adult and ready to greet Mitch with his favorite ginger beer that I kept my refrigerator stocked with for just this sort of spontaneous (yet regular) occurrence. Good thing I broke down and signed up for cable. We would lie on the sofa and watch TV until late at night. I supported the TV part to get to the sex part, which usually happened at two or three in the morning. Every now and then I would get up from the couch to make us something to eat. His thriftiness must have been rubbing off on me, because one evening in order to utilize some week-old cheese and day-old bread, I threw together something I called *mozzarella en carrozza* and which Mitch, a WASP with no continental inclinations whatsoever, couldn't pronounce. I figured this wasn't much different from grilled cheese and wouldn't overwhelm his naive palate. It was another resounding success.

～～～～～～～～

Italian Grilled Cheese for Teenage WASPs

Olive oil

Italian bread, or even a French baguette (1 to 2 days old is fine), thinly sliced

Mozzarella, thinly sliced (this may have been sitting around a couple of days, too)

1 to 2 eggs (depending on how much you are making), lightly beaten

Heat olive oil in a nonstick skillet over medium-high heat. Make little sandwiches with the bread and cheese and dip in the egg. When the olive oil is hot, slip in the sandwiches (you may insert a toothpick in each for the cooking if you find they are falling apart) and cook until golden on both sides and cheese is melted. Press with a kettle or pot full of water to flatten (if you've used toothpicks, remove them when the melted cheese has glued everything into place and press them then).

Yield: 1 loaf of bread makes 8 to 12 sandwiches.

There was much to be said for my new and altogether different lifestyle. I adapted easily to the role of teenager, especially since there were no parents in bed upstairs while we writhed around on the couch. Having never dated a teenager when that would have been appropriate, I relished getting a little taste late in life of what it might have felt like. What a drag that instead of school, I had to get up and go to work in the morning while Mitch could lie in bed. He would watch me dress as he dozed. "You look like a substitute teacher," he said, examining my outfit one morning. I was offended and brought it up in an e-mail later that day.

"No, no," he replied, "I meant like the substitute teacher that you lust after for the rest of your life." He'd leave handwritten notes around my apartment thanking me for the previous night's dinner or that morning's coffee. "Everything associated with you is delicious," read one.

These little things made him worth the trouble and filled me with hope that it would work out between us and we could buy a little house together in Williamsburg. Yes, I'd even live in Williamsburg if that was what was required.

Mitch spent his days in his apartment writing, though his career was at a bit of a standstill when we were together. His second novel, which was geared toward adults, was less successful than the first. A third novel, which had just come out from a San Francisco–based indie publisher, was about two teenage boys trying to get with the coolest teenage girl. I tried to persuade him to stick to young adult fiction, as that voice did come naturally to him. But Mitch argued—quite persuasively—that this meant giving up dreams of being the next John Updike, and he wasn't quite ready to let go of those. Mitch wrote all day long, and he wrote fast; he had boxes of novels for adults in his apartment, but he couldn't sell any of them.

One was a novel about a thirty-one-year-old woman who was loosely based on me. She used the same toiletries I did and even wore the same kinds of shoes. She was a woman riding high in her magazine career and was much more successful than I. She was a hard-ass, a tough boss, someone who yelled at people and got everything she wanted. Things Mitch imagined I was but I was not and never could be. I helped him to get that one in the hands of a few editors, having a personal stake in the project, even though it wasn't *really* me. No one bit.

Mitch liked visiting me at my real-life office, not just for the free office supplies and books I'd give him, but because he was excited about my work, even if I didn't have a car and driver to take me back and forth from it every day like that character he created. He was just as impressed that my job allowed me to talk to Harold Bloom on a daily basis, and what's more, to be addressed by him as "little bear" (which is what he called everyone he was fond of). Not only was Harold the smartest, but he was one of the kindest authors I ever worked with. I first got to know him during my Ethan days, and like the father I no longer had, he was extremely concerned about Ethan not stepping up to the connubial plate. "A very handsome fellow and quite smart," Harold declared in his deep, reflective, and just a tad British-accented tone, "but I fear he may be a mama's boy." The case wasn't quite as simple as Harold supposed, but I was honored by his concern.

Mitch supported me through two big career decisions. After I interviewed for the job I eventually took at *Harper's Magazine*, he came over to my apartment and spent an entire day with me weighing the pros and cons of the move. While I was on the phone with various advisers, including Professor Bloom, Mitch scribbled down questions for me to ask. Later, when I considered leaving *Harper's* for another magazine, I called Mitch, who was visiting his parents in Portland at the time, to agonize over the decision. There was no one better to discuss the dilemma with. Not that he was any less lost than I was over what to do, but he was as revved up as I was over the two phenomenal gigs I was forced to choose between. Mitch was totally there when I needed him for stuff like that.

Eventually, he came to terms with what seemed to be his calling and even had a dream agent in mind for the crossover. He sent her a new novel he hoped she would represent. When she phoned him to discuss some qualms she had with the manuscript, Mitch insisted on a meeting. He sat her and her staff down and explained to them what they weren't getting. They signed him on the spot. Did I mention he could be incredibly persuasive when he wanted to be?

There was another time that Mitch departed from the role of hapless teen he usually played and resembled the man of forty-two he actually was. This occurred on Sunday mornings when he hunkered down with *The New York Times'* "Mutual Funds Report" to see how his investments were faring. Though Mitch had no pending contracts when we were dating, he was by no means broke. He had a bunch of money in the bank from the advance, royalties, and movie deal from his first book. But instead of spending it, he invested it in mutual funds. How many men can introduce a girl to electroclash *and* the index fund? Seven years later, my Ladytron CD gathers dust and my Vanguard account steadily loses value. I'll stick with the latter despite the current volatility. I may toss the CD; I never really liked it anyway.

Mitch kept his overhead low, his rent was cheap, and his Brooks Brothers oxford-cloth shirts came from the Salvation Army (though he did spend on "tennis shoes," as he called them; it was important to have the correct Adidas or Pumas). He would stop to consider any old shoes or clothing that neighbors left out on their stoops to give away (a brownstone Brooklyn custom) or those, most likely stolen from cars, that drug addicts sold in the Second Avenue subway station. I suspected he did this mainly to get a rise out of me, so I encouraged him. "Yes, those shoes *do* look really nice, go ahead, try them on," I would say. When I wasn't feeding him, he was at home eating hot dogs. One rare night I spent at his place, I made us a frittata with eggs and frozen peas from the bodega on the corner. Mitch said grace before we ate, thanking God for me and for his new agent.

～～～ ～～ ～～

Frugal Frittata

> 1 cup frozen peas (or fresh if you are lucky
>   enough to have them—Mitch never was)
> Salt
> 1 tablespoon butter
> 1 tablespoon olive oil
> 1 small red onion, chopped
> 6 eggs
> Freshly ground pepper
> 1/4 cup freshly grated parmigiano

Fill a medium saucepan halfway with water, put on high heat, and bring to a simmer. Add peas and a little salt and cook for 5 minutes. Drain and set aside to cool.

Melt the butter with the oil in a cast-iron or other ovenproof skillet over medium heat, add the onions, and cook until almost soft.

Preheat broiler.

Lightly beat the eggs, then stir in salt, pepper, parmigiano, and the cooled peas. Turn up the heat a bit on the onions and then add the eggs; allow them to set, then stir once or twice with a wooden spoon. Once the bottom is firm, put the pan under the broiler and cook until the top is golden, 3 to 4 more minutes. Watch constantly—with broiling, there are only a few seconds standing between beautifully golden and terribly burned.

Remove from the oven and allow the frittata to rest for a minute or two. Serve in the skillet or flip onto a plate.

Yield: 4 servings.

I invited Mitch to spend Thanksgiving with my family in Connecticut. His only other option was to have dinner with a group of old men from AA. Or so he said. Mitch was expert at downgrading his friends, his family, himself, and most of the situations he found himself in. I thought it was a pose; maybe it's what he really believed. He debated his answer for three days. Then he called, his voice shuddering with fear. "I want to come to your house for Thanksgiving."

Time to focus on yet another dilemma: what Mitch should bring my mother as a gift. I wanted her to like Mitch, so this was a dilemma for me as well.

"She likes chocolate," I said.

"But I don't know what kind to get."

I had Mitch come meet me at La Maison du Chocolat, which was across the street from my office. Everything at La Maison du Chocolat costs a fortune. In fact, the very idea of Mitch Smith standing inside La Maison du Chocolat makes me giggle, even now as I'm writing, but impressing my mother was more important than a few moments of discomfort for Mitch in a fancy French chocolate shop. It took a good twenty minutes of scanning the shelves before we found something suitable that was pretty but wouldn't break Mitch's fiercely protected bank: a big block of baking chocolate. Presenting it to my mother was another trauma Mitch couldn't handle, so I did it for him as he stood by. I explained that it was very fine baking chocolate but that she could just break off a piece and eat if she wanted to, just as the saleswoman at the store told us. My mother was delighted. So was Mitch.

At dinner, my family asked how we met.

"I got this big crush on her at a party three years ago, but she didn't notice me. When she had nothing else going on, she called me," Mitch announced.

Mitch didn't much like following Ethan. He knew I'd wanted to marry my last boyfriend because he'd probed me about the reason for our split and I'd told him the truth. I'd also tried to tell him that Ethan and I hadn't worked out because Mitch was my "destiny."

"I'm not your destiny!" he said. "I'm just the last guy left on the bench who gets called to the field because there's no one left to play. 'Hey, you, you're short and you're not the best player, but you'll have to do,' the coach yells. 'Get out there!'"

Truthfully, in those days the only time I thought about Ethan was when Mitch was acting out. Then I would think to myself, Thanks, Ethan, thanks for throwing me to the dogs like this. Yes, in the beginning I was thrilled to have Mitch to throw into Ethan's face—the desire for vendetta does run in the Sicilian half of my blood, I'm afraid—but now I was discovering that Mitch could make me happy in ways that Ethan never could. The two of them may as well have been from different planets, with me adapting to each wildly diverse way of life while inhabiting their respective terrains. Mitch made me aware of the myriad things that Ethan couldn't give. The sex, for instance: Not to say that Ethan and I didn't have a fine sex life, we did; we had a fine sex life. But let's just say that Ethan was squeamish in ways that Mitch was not. I am pleased that I got to experience the kind of passion I had with Mitch. Of course, I didn't know what I was missing out on when I was with Ethan. But that's just it: We don't know what's in store, so really there is no reason to get too upset about losing anything, not that you could ever convince anyone in the throes of loss of this, certainly not me, who moaned about Ethan months after our breakup.

Mitch is the only man I ever dated who got jealous, or at least admitted to the feeling. I found this refreshing. I cringe at the thought of any of my boyfriends' exes and ruminated often upon Mitch's. I could tell Ethan every romantic detail of my getting together with Kit and he wouldn't flinch. Mitch didn't want to know the story, and he didn't want to meet Kit. One afternoon, before a meeting with a prospective editor at my company, Mitch stopped by my office, where he noticed an e-mail from Ethan on my computer screen. He didn't mention it at the time, but he didn't call me after his appointment so I knew something was up. The next morning, he sent an e-mail telling me what he saw. "I was sitting across from my editor and all I could think about was: Why is that guy still e-mailing her? What is going on? Is she using me to try to leverage him into marrying her? She's never said they still talked or stayed in contact. I tell her about all my interactions with my exes."

Ethan and I weren't in touch. I just happened to run into him on the subway that morning and he wrote to apologize for being "a little out of it."

Even something as insignificant as parsley could set Mitch off. One evening, I was chopping a bunch, my twelve-inch cutting board teetering back and forth on my six-inch counter. The racket upset Mitch. He thought I was acting out anger directed at him. I had my share of reasons to be annoyed with Mitch, but I wasn't just then, I merely like my parsley to look good.

Barring the occasional noisy run-in

with an herb, things were going pretty well with us through the holiday season. Mitch asked me to join his family at their vacation home in Mexico for Christmas. Though I'd spent a great deal of time with the Binders and saw it add up to nothing, I viewed this invitation as a sign of seriousness on Mitch's part. I accepted immediately and didn't allow myself to fret about the plane ticket, which, because I bought it somewhere close to the last minute, cost more than any I had purchased before. Mitch went home to Portland for a couple of weeks before Christmas and flew down to Mexico from there. I stayed in New York to eat lobsters and many other sea creatures on Christmas Eve with my family, then got on a plane at five a.m. on Christmas morning. By two p.m., I was lying on the beach in Mexico with Mitch, drinking Fanta and listening to Joseph Arthur on my iPod. The Smiths' house, white stucco with a terra-cotta roof, was surrounded by flowers; behind it was a little bridge that crossed a canal and led to the ocean. Mitch and I had our own little suite downstairs with a private bathroom where lizards scurried around at night. The house was part of a community where a number of the Smiths' neighbors from Portland had vacation homes. Mitch's mother and father were there, as were his sister and brother-in-law and their two young sons.

Mitch's mother made a turkey from the Costco in Puerto Vallarta for Christmas dinner. It was a little dry, but the view of the Pacific Ocean I took in while eating it moistened it right up. I brought the Smiths a bunch of my mother's Christmas cookies and a big box of chocolates from Jacques Torres that Mrs. Smith put on a shelf in the kitchen but never touched. Mitch said they were afraid of those chocolates, that, like Daisy Buchanan with Jay Gatsby's shirts, they had never seen such beautiful chocolates in their lives. But that was all just part of Mitch's act. Still, they never opened the chocolate, and I have no better explanation.

The Smiths were vigilant about not drinking Mexican water. We used the bottled stuff for everything, even to brush our teeth. "And make sure you keep your mouth firmly closed when you're in the shower," Mrs. Smith instructed, sealing her lips tightly after saying it to demonstrate. Vegetables were verboten. So much for the wonderful street food I'd heard about; the Smiths looked at me as though I were crazy when I mentioned it. Mitch's mother and sister enjoyed going to the outdoor market to check out the locals and the produce, but they never considered buying it. It never occurred to them that blanching vegetables in boiling water would make them safe for us to eat. Embracing my enterprising idea, Mrs. Smith bought string beans and potatoes, which I boiled and dressed with olive oil, garlic, and a little vinegar; we ate them with steaks that Dr. Smith had stockpiled in a giant freezer. He would mix us vodka-and-orange-juice cocktails—"toddies," he called them—while I cooked.

~~~~~~~~~~

String Bean and Potato Salad for Gringos

> 1 pound string beans (or long beans or green beans or whatever you call them)
> 1 pound baby red potatoes
> 1 clove garlic, minced
> 2 tablespoons extra-virgin olive oil
> 1 teaspoon red wine vinegar
> 1/2 teaspoon salt
> Freshly ground pepper

Put two big pots of water on the stove and bring them to a boil. Meanwhile, pull the ends off the string beans and halve the potatoes. When the water is boiling, add the vegetables each to its own pot. The beans will take about 6 minutes, the potatoes will take 12 to 15. Test them both to see if they are done to your liking. The string beans should be soft but still have a little snap to them. When this is determined, remove the beans with a slotted spoon or drain them in a colander, then run a little cold water over them to stop the cooking—or better yet, dump them in a large bowl filled with water and ice and drain them again. This will stop them from cooking and give them a bright color. You can allow the vegetables to cool or season them now, combining both with garlic, oil, vinegar, salt, and pepper.

Yield: 6 to 8 servings.

Mitch's sister Penelope was going through some marital tensions with her husband, Michael, when we were all down there. Mitch and I didn't need to know what the problem was; as soon as we noticed him wearing a T-shirt that advocated "juggling for peace," we had all the explanation we needed, as well as a source of laughter for years to come. Someone that earnest would never survive with a Smith. Earnest, too, was the family in its endeavors to make peace between this couple, so much so that they were willing to take a real risk and let us go out to a restaurant for dinner to celebrate Michael's birthday. As long as we kept away from lettuce and ice cubes, Mrs. Smith surmised that we would be all right. We weren't. In the middle of the night, Mitch and I were struck by the expected unpleasantness. He succumbed first: I woke up in the middle of the night to find him gone. He wasn't in the bed, he wasn't in our bathroom.

"Using the bathroom down here would be too much sharing," Mitch explained when he returned. "I thought introducing you to my parents and my dog were enough for this trip." Not long after Mitch, I was stricken. I was in so much pain that I fainted on the bathroom floor. Mitch had to bust in and rescue me. Talk about sharing! And yet as embarrassing as this all sounds, it wasn't. Our illness was bonding, and I was moved by Mitch's care and heroism. (Not to mention the blatant contrast it revealed between him and Ethan: If I had ever passed out on a bathroom floor under my last boyfriend's watch, he would have just left me to die while he lay in bed with his eye pillow over his face.) My illness humanized me for Mitch. Finally, I wasn't "perfect," he said.

Mitch and I were on separate flights back to New York on New Year's Eve. When we parted at the airport in Mexico, Mitch said, "I'll call you when I get home." So 2002 dawned with me wishing good health and fortune to the taxi driver who was taking me home from Newark. I checked my messages all night. Mitch never called.

Silly me to think that trip would mark the end of Mitch's unpredictable behavior. Figuring that if an AeroMéxico plane went down somewhere over the Carolinas I probably would have heard about it, I held out until about two o'clock on New Year's Day before I called him to call him on not calling. He didn't take it well, and we didn't speak again for a couple of days, during which Mitch forwarded me some e-mails from his mother exclaiming how much the family liked me. I liked them, too. I could see myself fitting in as a Smith and had spent my plane ride happily doing so. That was before he didn't call.

Mitch thought it was awfully literal of me to get all bent out of shape over him not calling when he got home just because he'd said, "I'll call you when I get home." We went to his favorite Chinatown restaurant, Sweet-n-Tart, to discuss it. I loved that place, with its noodle soups and scallion pancakes and checks that never came to more than $14. I went there even without Mitch. Their menu included a list of sweet teas that were supposed to contain healing properties. Each flavor was paired with the ailment it was meant to soothe. Unfortunately, there was none claiming to alleviate the confusion of being with a guy you are deeply drawn to, who goes out of his way to exasperate.

We made it through winter relatively smoothly. We went to movies, and Mitch even paid sometimes. "I like paying for you," he said in a voice tinged with amazement. On a cold and rainy Sunday, we went to the half-price matinee of *The Royal Tenenbaums*. I snuck in a thermos of coffee brewed just the way Mitch liked it. The movie dazzled, with Luke Wilson, an astonishing sound track, and the mink coat Fendi designed especially for Gwyneth Paltrow's role. It was a paean to hipsterism even I could love. When we got back to my apartment, we snuggled on the sofa and Mitch kissed my face one hundred times, counting every one.

I was by now solidly opposed to eating Valentine's Day dinner in a restaurant, and good thing, too. I couldn't fathom sitting with Mitch, enjoying the candlelight prix fixe à deux. Still, having spent my share of V-Days alone or out for dinner with my widowed mother, I always insist on celebrating the holiday whenever there's a man in my picture, however tenuous. But what to serve Mitch? Champagne was out. He wouldn't give a damn for oysters or caviar. No, simple meat and potatoes was the way to go for him. When I announced that I would be making pot roast, he questioned my wisdom. But I didn't let it deter me; I couldn't make heads or tails of Mitch's mind when it came to us, but I could ascertain the needs of his palate, and pot roast with gravy was what it craved. I was right. Mitch said it was the best thing he had ever eaten in his life. He got a lot of things right that evening. He showed up at the door dressed in a coat and tie (from the thrift store, of course) and carrying a bouquet (of carnations, but still).

"This is the first time I ever bought flowers for a girl," he said.

The chocolate layer cake I made for dessert was to be a soft rose color, but the tiniest drop of food coloring immediately turned the confection the hottest pink. It was awfully girly, but Mitch didn't mind girly; the cover of his first novel was hot pink. Nor did he comment on the fact that it was over-frosted and lopsided. He finished every morsel. It warmed my baker's heart.

~~~~~~~~~~~

Mitch's Mother Is a Yankee Pot Roast

1 (3- to 4-pound) chuck or rump roast
Salt and pepper
2 tablespoons olive oil
2 carrots
2 celery stalks
1 medium onion
1 clove garlic
1 cup dry red wine
1 cup beef broth
1 tablespoon tomato paste
1 bay leaf
A few sprigs of thyme or 1 teaspoon dried
    thyme
1/2 pound egg noodles
1 tablespoon butter
1 tablespoon chopped parsley

Season the meat with salt and pepper. Heat olive oil in a Dutch oven over medium-high heat. Brown meat on all sides, letting it develop a good crust, about 5 minutes per side.

While meat is browning, finely chop the carrots, celery, onion, and garlic. If you have a food processor, cut the vegetables into small pieces, throw them in, and give them a good whirl.

When the meat is browned, remove it from the Dutch oven, then add the chopped vegetables and a little more oil if needed. Cook the vegetables with a little salt until they are soft and browned a bit, 5 to 10 minutes. Add the wine and broth, scraping up the brown bits that have accumulated around the pot. Return the meat to the pot and bring it all to a simmer. Add the tomato paste, bay leaf, and thyme, lower heat, and cover pot. Cook for 3 hours, turning the roast every 30 minutes or so for even cooking.

When time is up, remove the roast to a cutting board and tent it with foil. Strain the juices from the pot and reduce them in a small saucepan (you may add some butter if you like). Cook the egg noodles according to directions on the package. Drain them, add butter, slice the meat, and serve over the noodles covered with sauce and sprinkled with chopped parsley.

Serves 2, with enough for sandwiches the next day.

～～ ～～ ～～ ～～

Hot Pink Cake

(Adapted from the Hershey's cocoa can)

For the cake

- 2 cups sugar
- 1 3/4 cups all-purpose flour
- 3/4 cups cocoa powder (the better the quality, the better the cake; I am devoted to Valrhona, but Hershey's is fine)
- 1 1/2 teaspoons baking soda
- 1 1/2 teaspoons baking powder
- 1 teaspoon salt

2 eggs, left out of the fridge for about 30 minutes
1 stick butter, melted and cooled slightly
1 cup whole milk
2 teaspoons vanilla
1 cup boiling water

Preheat oven to 350 degrees. Generously butter and flour two 8-inch baking pans and line with parchment paper.

In a large mixing bowl, stir together the dry ingredients. Add eggs, butter, milk, and vanilla and beat at medium speed for 2 to 3 minutes, until all ingredients are combined and the cocoa bits are smoothed out. Stir in the boiling water. Pour batter into pans and bake at 350 degrees until a cake tester comes out with moist crumbs, 30 to 35 minutes. Cool 10 minutes in pans, then transfer to cooling racks. Wait until the cakes have cooled completely before frosting.

For the frosting:

1 stick very soft butter

1 pound confectioners' sugar
3 to 4 tablespoons milk
1 teaspoon vanilla
A little too much red food dye

Mix all ingredients with an electric mixer at low speed until creamy. Add more milk if necessary. The trick is for the icing to be not too thin and not too goopy.

Something always goes wrong for me aesthetically when I make this cake, but it's always delicious.

Yield: enough for one 8-inch cake or 24 cupcakes.

Our first real breakup happened after Mitch and I spent a day with his friend Francine, a hipster from Portland who was well over the age and weight requirements for the job. Francine had come to New York to nurse her mother, who was recovering from an operation. Mitch and I took the train up to New Rochelle to see her.

"Mom, Mitch is here!" Francine yelled

to her mother in her sickroom upstairs when we arrived. "Say hello to Mom," she commanded Mitch.

"Hello, Mrs. Simon," Mitch shouted dutifully.

We spent the day touring Westchester thrift shops, beginning with the Entenmann's bakery store, where we picked up three boxes of chocolate-covered doughnuts for a dollar each. Francine found a fantastic blue silk dress for me at the enormous Salvation Army in Portchester. Then we went back to Francine's mother's house, where we drank coffee and ate doughnuts. "Say good-bye to Mom," Francine directed Mitch before she drove us back to the station.

"Good-bye, Mrs. Simon," said Mitch as we walked out the screen door.

Mitch seemed unusually quiet on the train ride home, but I figured Francine had just talked him out. From Grand Central Station we walked to the 42nd Street subway, the same station where Mitch and I parted after our first date. We found ourselves at the iron fence where we'd kissed for the first time eight months earlier. We recreated the moment, then kissed some more on the subway platform. When we got to my apartment, Mitch slumped onto the couch, tears in his eyes. "You don't like my friends."

"I was nice to Francine!" I said. "Didn't I make a big fuss over the dress she found for me?" I did—it was a fantastic dress and it fit me perfectly; I wore it until it shredded.

Mitch left the next morning; the box of doughnuts he left behind was the one sweet thing in a harsh week. I ate one every morning. My mother always used to keep those doughnuts around the house for my family when we were little, but a box never lasted more than a day, so I never knew that Entenmann's chocolate-covered doughnuts ripen. They got more and more delicious with every passing day.

After a couple of days, I got the usual post-AA-meeting call from Mitch, but this time he didn't ask to come over; he wanted to meet me for coffee.

I knew this was the end.

I checked out my face in the mirror before I left my apartment, wondering how I was supposed to look for such an occasion. Does your makeup have to be perfect when you're about to be dumped? On my way to Halcyon, a coffee bar/record store/vintage furniture store (the most Williamsburgesque place in my neighborhood), I felt like dead man walking.

Mitch was there first with his coffee. I got one for myself and then sat down. We made a little small talk, and then Mitch launched into what I knew was coming. "I think we should break up," he said, but he was crying while he said it. Then he launched into happy memories: "I think of us going to a movie with a thermos of coffee in a tote bag," he said as he wept.

"But why are you breaking up with me if it's making you cry?" I said. "Obviously, there's some depth of feeling there. I think you need to come to terms with your need for me."

"I know I have needs [*sic*] for you," he whined, "and I've been trying, but I just can't do it."

I alternated between comforting him and trying to convince him that he could do it. I even brought up my dream of our little house in Williamsburg. "You could use your money for the down payment, and I could pay the mortgage with my salary." Is there anyone in the world besides me who would introduce a phantasmagoric real estate arrangement into a breakup conversation?

There were no more doughnuts and no more Mitch. Those first few nights, I would get into my bed and scream into my pillow in agony. In the daytime, I would wonder where he was. On Sunday afternoon, I knew he'd be at a bar in Red Hook where he was scheduled to read.

I wasn't allowed to go there. His places weren't my places anymore.

But a party for our friend Henry was just as much my place as his. It hurt so much to see Mitch there that I ended up bolting early to take solace in my sofa and a pack of American Spirit Lights (even though I hadn't smoked for about two years) with Ginia, who came with me to the party. My despair was premature. The next day, Mitch wrote to me, and we saw each other a few days later. We were going to be friends. We went out and shared a tray of fruit and cheese, and being friends was fun; we were getting along.

"Isn't it much easier to be friends with me?" Mitch said when I left him at the subway.

Yes, it was. My despair over our breakup had been replaced with a quiet contentment over our newfound status. Then one night Mitch came over to watch TV after one such date, and the next thing you knew he was trying to kiss me. "What are you doing?" I said.

"I don't know," he replied.

It was impossible for us to be friends. Friends with benefits, on the other hand, continued for another year. I took him to a dinner where his hero, John Updike, spoke; he took me to Mexico again. But whenever I felt some glimmer of hope that maybe things could work out between us, Mitch would shoot me down. One day I got an e-mail that went something like this:

> **Hey G,**
> **I know we hung out and had sex or whatever, but I don't feel like having a girlfriend right now.**
> **M.**

I wrote:

> **I do not wish to speak to you ever again.**

I pretty much kept my promise. Okay, maybe we slept together once a year or two later. And we are occasionally in touch now. In the time that we weren't speaking, Mitch, who didn't want a girl-friend or whatever, got married. He also got a lot of books published and another movie deal. He didn't grow up, but that might be a good career move for him.

~~~ ~~~ ~~~

Marcus Caldwell Ate and Ran

~~~ ~~~ ~~~

I'm going to marry that woman" was all I needed to hear. I had seen him stretching and preening before our softball game, but really, you couldn't miss Marcus, his white hair sticking straight up, his Wayfarer eyeglass frames, his Kermit-the-Frog green sneakers. He was a man well into middle age, with an arty style that made him someone I might consider, though actually I wasn't considering him until I got wind of the fact that he wanted to marry me.

It was the first time in history that *Harper's Magazine* won a softball game against our perceived literary rival, *The New*

Yorker, and our scrappy team (dressed in our own T-shirts and hats, as opposed to our opponents decked out in logo'd garb supplied by their corporate owner) was in a great mood. As public relations director, I took the opportunity to boost internal morale and show the competition what terrific sports we were, by offering to buy both winners and losers drinks on my expense account at Tap a Keg, a bar not far from Central Park. Marcus was sitting catty-corner from me at the bar, talking to Elizabeth, one of our editors. I was across from them, eating popcorn and talking to the summer interns. Marcus kept looking over at me, smiling, waving, and mouthing, "Thank you," while toasting me with his beer. When I got up to mingle, Elizabeth told me that he was asking about me. "Who is that woman? I'm going to marry her," he reportedly kept saying over and over.

I went outside where the smokers, Marcus among them, convened. I bummed a cigarette from him and introduced myself. Marcus was a cartoonist; I asked him to describe some of his cartoons for me. He talked me through one involving a couple in bed and a bicycle helmet. I didn't get the joke. "That's often the case," he said with winning self-deprecation. I was on my way out, so we didn't talk long; he gave me his card with his signature emblazoned upon it along with the usual pertinent details, and I gave him mine. I went back inside to say good night to my colleagues, and as I was leaving, Marcus, who was sitting on a bench with some others in front of the bar, shouted, "Good night, Giulia!" His voice had a Charles Nelson Reilly ring to it, full of character, with a slightly gay undertone.

My plan had been to take the summer off from dating. In early spring, a few weeks after I said good-bye to Mitch for the last time (well, pretty much the last time—I don't count random sexual encounters years apart, and neither should anyone else), I met a handsome Indian of British extraction on the subway. He asked me the time and kept on talking. He said he was a journalist. I gave him my card. I wasn't averse to the idea of a relationship initiated on the subway—in fact, I believed that public transportation was a perfectly fine place to meet people. My friend Monica Mahoney married a doctor with an MBA whom she met on the M103 bus, and that wasn't the only story I knew; however, the man I met turned out to be exactly the type of person one might expect to find on the subway. Though he was good-looking and wore nice clothes, I came to learn that his journalism career consisted of one radio piece for the BBC sometime in the early nineties. Kam didn't do anything. I assumed (and hoped) he was supporting himself with family money, but I eventually discovered that the Upper East Side apartment where I dropped him off in a cab after our second date was not his. After a couple of weeks of dating, he admitted that he was living with a woman. When I called to tell him I was not interested in seeing him again, his solution was to put me on the phone with her.

Before I could protest, there she was telling me that Kam and I had a good thing going and she didn't want to get in the way.

When I relayed this bizarre incident to Jen, she was so disturbed that she urged me to come and stay with her and Jeff for a few days in case the guy was dangerous (I stayed home and emerged unscathed). Ginia had given up on my sanity completely. I was due for a period of soul-searching. Up till this point in my life, I had considered myself an adept judge of character; now I wasn't so sure. The heartbreak of Ethan and whatever that thing was with Mitch had corrupted whatever insight I may have possessed. I was becoming a type I have never been and never wanted to be: a woman who will date anyone just to be dating someone.

An e-mail from Marcus Caldwell was waiting for me when I arrived at work the morning after our meeting.

Giulia,
You left too early last night.
I would like to take you out and buy
you 82 drinks.
Are you free tonight or tomorrow
night?
Marcus

And with that, my period of reflection ended. I wanted to go on a date with Marcus. I wanted to go on a date with Marcus that night. It wasn't the mild concern that accepting for that evening would make me look a bit easy to win that gave me pause, it was more the fact that I wasn't dressed for a date. Tired from the previous evening's revels, I had rolled out of bed and, without much thought, had thrown on a simple skirt and T-shirt. Back in my closet in Brooklyn was a brand-new dress I briefly considered wearing before deciding this unremarkable outfit better suited my state of mind. Boy, was I sorry I hadn't opted for that blue silk jersey sheath with the bamboo pattern!

After a few phone consultations with the usual suspects, I resolved that a quick trip to Brooklyn and back was not such a big deal. I'd leave work early and take care of some other errands, too. Marcus let me know that he'd be riding down from Harlem on his Vespa. I didn't disclose the elaborate maneuvers I would be employing to arrive at Blue Ribbon, a SoHo restaurant popular with chefs and bon vivants. Marcus was most definitely the latter, albeit an aging one.

When I arrived he was standing by the entry, already halfway through a glass of white wine. I was a little put off by how old he looked out of his softball clothes and dressed in a blue button-down shirt and well-worn khakis. Once my eyes adjusted to the white hair and the wrinkles and perhaps aided by my getting a glass of wine of my own, I was able to relax in his company. This took all of five minutes. We brought our glasses to a table near the bar and ordered a dozen oysters, a *spécialité de la maison*. I listened to the story of Marcus's recently dissolved family life. He had two children in their twenties, both in New York City. When they were little the whole clan spent a few years in a villa near Lucca, where Marcus painted and his wife gardened; thus the Vespa and Marcus's penchant for things Italian. His daughter now lived in Queens with her boyfriend; his son was an actor who was also a drummer in a band that was playing nearby that evening. Would I like to go see them? You bet! We settled up and Marcus showed me to his mint green Vespa; he had a matching mint green helmet, and there was a little black companion helmet stowed under the seat for me. I hopped on, gingerly wrapping my arms around Marcus's waist, a little uncomfortable with the accelerated intimacy enforced by this mode of travel. Marcus's cotton shirt was soft, his midsection pleasingly taut, and there is a lot to be said for cruising around Greenwich Village on the back of a Vespa on one of the first evenings of summer. I was seduced, which was, no doubt, the intention behind the acquisition. That Vespa took ten years off him.

Marcus introduced me to his son, who was quite good-looking, even with the Mohawk he was sporting for a role in a student film. At Kenny's Castaways, we drank Brooklyn Lager and listened to the band. They played some kind of country rock, my least favorite kind. I sat there imagining myself stepmother to this young man who was closer to my age than I was to his father's. Oddly, the fantasy was not unpleasant; I had come quite a distance in two hours. Thing was, I had a remarkable ability for turning any picture into the picture I wanted to see: me with a husband. My imagination had the flexibility of a thirteen-year-old Chinese gymnast.

The band finished up around midnight. Marcus and I made one more stop for hamburgers and red wine at Florent, a pioneering restaurant disguised as an old diner in Manhattan's now too trendy Meatpacking District. Florent (which closed in 2008, breaking many a New Yorker's heart) was open all night, catering to the city's club-goers and transvestites. Though we were neither, it was the only place I could think of that would serve us food at that hour. After our late night repast, Marcus and I sailed over the Brooklyn Bridge on the Vespa, landing in front of my house, where Marcus lingered, showing me photos of his paintings, which he stored in the same compartment where the helmet was. He kept a *Zagat* guide in there, too, for picking restaurants on the fly. The artwork was okay, but by now I was so determined to like this man that I convinced myself they were more than okay and that, in fact, he was an undiscovered Max Beckmann. We kissed on my stoop, and I went through that initial adjustment again. Pulling away from a kiss and being confronted with so many wrinkles was jarring, sort of like kissing my father. At thirty-seven, I was hardly an ingenue, though, and Marcus seemed so excited about me that I couldn't help but get a little giddy myself.

"Missed you while riding home on the FDR Drive last night," said the next morning's e-mail.

Marcus thoughtfully chose a Brooklyn restaurant I raved about on our first date as the location for our second two days later. We met first for a drink on the Lower East Side, a bar he picked that I had never heard of. For someone twenty years older than me, Marcus sure knew his downtown hangouts. After a couple of glasses of red wine, we headed to Brooklyn on the Vespa. As we waited for a stoplight at the exit of the Brooklyn Bridge, people stared at us from their cars admiringly. We must have looked like a pretty neat couple, arty Marcus with his crazy white hair sticking up on his head and me in a light pink cashmere sweater over a shiny bias-cut skirt. I wouldn't have to cook for Marcus; I was already providing a great service to him by bestowing my youth to his funky-old-man scene. I liked what this liaison did for my image, too. It added a bohemian dimension that had hitherto been lacking from my profile.

At Locanda Vini & Olii in Fort Greene, we took a table outside. The talk turned to past relationships, a frequent conversational detour in early dates. Marcus was just out of one, with someone, it turned out, I had met. This sort of happenstance is not uncommon in New York City, which is a lot more like Mayberry than you would believe, at least in the circles I travel in. We all know one another, and I would venture to say that the degree of sexual separation between me and everyone I know hovers at around one. Renee Lachaise had been deflowered by my friend Conrad Peterson a few years before. I knew much more about that ordeal than I wanted to both then and especially now. I started to work out her age in my head, and no matter how many calculations I made, I could not arrive at a comforting total. She had to be at least ten years younger than me. Marcus and Renee had a long affair before he left his wife and exurban homestead to hole up with her in five hundred square feet on the Upper West Side. Now that I knew he'd dated someone even younger than me, the feeling of being the trophy babe on the eccentric artist's Vespa was gone. The revelation took some of the wind out of my scooter-velocity-blown sails.

But not so much that I didn't invite Marcus back to my place for Prosecco. I didn't say sex, I said Prosecco! "What if I carried you into the bedroom and made love to you?" Marcus said when we were drinking it and fooling around on the sofa. But I refused his Rhett Butler–infused suggestion. I may have ended my moratorium on dating, but I was going to take it slow this time.

So slow, in fact, that within the hour I had invited him to Connecticut for the upcoming Fourth of July weekend, where he would meet my mother and Aunt Marie and we'd probably end up sharing a bed. The number of men who would agree to such an expedition five days into knowing someone is infinitesimal. But Marcus counted among that tiny minority. In my mind, he exhibited a refreshing lack of neuroses rare in New York City, where everyone overconsiders everything. The typical male of the thirty-something variety, at least, would shy away from such an invitation, fearing it would imply commitment. Yet another selling point for the (much) older man!

"I'm coming to Connecticut and I'm bringing a man who is closer to your age than to mine," I told my mother on the telephone the next morning. I knew she wouldn't mind; whatever would get me to Connecticut for a weekend was all right with her. I could be bringing a recently paroled Charles Manson and her only concern would be whether or not he was still a vegetarian.

"Good," she replied without missing a beat. "I always thought you needed someone older."

I met Marcus at his Harlem apartment after work; we'd pick up his car and drive to Connecticut from there. Marcus lived in a slummy building in a grim part of town, but I embraced its tattered appeal. There was marble somewhere under the dirt on that lobby floor, and Marcus had a considerable amount of space, not to mention some excellent views of the Hudson River and northern New Jersey. I imagined hosting big parties up here. Marcus told me he had recently thrown one featuring oysters and beer. I didn't know how to shuck and wondered if this would be a problem.

The walls of the apartment were covered with Marcus's paintings, and stacks of them lined the hallways. "We can bring some of these over to your place and hang them there," he offered. I liked that idea. What I didn't like was the eight-by-ten photo of him and Renee Lachaise on the wall in his studio, and what I detested was the framed e-mail from Renee Lachaise hanging near his bed. "I love you," it read. However, I resolutely ignored those displays and concentrated on my oyster-shucking dilemma. I certainly didn't say anything to Marcus; that would mean acknowledging them to myself. Anyway, lots of people have the ability to move on fast, even faster than it takes to remove relationship ephemera from walls. I was counting on Marcus to be one of those.

We grabbed some CDs for the drive. I had brought some of my own, too.

"This is so fresh!" Marcus exclaimed in his emphatic voice whenever I played my music.

I also brought *Super Hits of the Seventies*, figuring that would appeal, but Marcus seemed to have missed groups from that period like Supertramp and ELO, the ones I liked. He may have been busy raising his children. Or maybe we just had different tastes.

My mother and Aunt Marie came out to the front porch to meet Marcus when we drove up in his beat-up car. "Hello, ladies!" he chanted, greeting them with the warmth and ebullience that had worked wonders on me. He'd do fine with my family, I thought as I proudly showed him the house and then the table on the back deck. My mother, who had been getting a little slack with her cooking, pulled off a remarkable dinner in anticipation of what she probably imagined and hoped was a sophisticated older gentleman. Marcus seemed to enchant the matriarchy, and I felt so comfortable that I couldn't believe we had met only a few days earlier.

~~~ ~~~ ~~~ ~~~

Dinner to Impress an Older Gentleman

Grilled Marinated Flank Steak

2 to 3 pounds flank steak

1/4 cup olive oil

1/4 cup red wine vinegar

1 garlic glove, minced

1 teaspoon dried oregano

1/2 teaspoon salt

Freshly ground pepper

Place meat in a bowl or Ziploc bag with remaining ingredients and marinate for 30 minutes on the counter and as much as overnight in the refrigerator.

Preheat broiler or grill. Cook for 4 to 5 minutes on each side for medium-rare. Slice thinly.

Yield: 4 to 6 servings.

～～～～～～～～～～

Fried Red Potatoes

1 pound baby red potatoes
1 tablespoon olive oil
1 tablespoon butter
Salt

Place potatoes in a large pot, cover with water, and bring to a boil. Cook for about 15 minutes, until almost tender. Drain, let potatoes cool a bit, then cut them into quarters.

In a large heavy skillet over medium-high heat, add the olive oil and butter. When the butter is bubbling, add the potatoes and cook until browned on each of their skinless sides, about 7 minutes per side.

Drain on paper towels, sprinkle with salt.

Serves 4.

Now that he had met my mother and Aunt Marie, was there a point in hiding anything from Marcus? I had some reasons to be prudent—the fact that we had just met, the lingering Renee Lachaise-iana around his apartment—but I didn't heed them. He was at my house, I had a brand-new hot pink leopard-print negligee (classier than it sounds) from the same designer who made that blue dress with the bamboo pattern, and it did some nice things for my curves. "Your body is one I've always dreamed of but never saw," Marcus said. His wasn't too bad, either, better than most of the thirty-year-olds I've known. "I worked in a rock quarry every summer when I was a teenager, and it just stayed with me," he said when I asked him how this was possible. Knowing what I know now, I don't think he was telling the truth, but at the time, I was brimming with acceptance and appreciation.

We got up at dawn and went to the beach; it was a revelation to be there so early. Who knew that the sun rises right there on Long Island Sound and people come out to greet it with jumping, yapping dogs? I looked back to the previous Saturday, which I had spent at home alone, watching the women's finals of the French Open while gloomily eating the grilled salmon with lemon-tarragon butter I used to make for Ethan. At the supermarket, I had run into a friend of Mitch's, which didn't help to alleviate all the pain I was feeling over this recent breakup. I would never have predicted that one week later I'd be having an amorous weekend with this kooky guy who was introducing me to pleasures I had never known in a place I had been to countless times. I never noticed how the smell of salt water pervaded our house until Marcus pointed it out to me. We swam at high tide at beaches I had never visited. We found two Adirondack chairs perched in front of one of the Mc-Mansions that seemed to be replacing all the cottages along the shore ("Gatsby's house," Marcus called it) and made them our own. We'd sit in them for a pre-dinner cocktail of Coronas with lime. Marcus photographed every moment with his digital camera. My mother handled the cooking.

"This is the best weekend of my life!" Marcus exclaimed over and over. When I was back at the office on Tuesday, he called me first thing to reiterate the sentiment. "Thank you for the best weekend of my life!"

In retrospect, this was a bit of an insult to his children. Could a weekend with me and my mother and Aunt Marie really be as good as the first weekend at home with a newborn? Granted that must be a stressful time, but there's got to be some wonder to it that is far grander than discovering my body or Aunt Marie's waffles.

An early summer heat wave postponed my cooking for Marcus. Even I have limits and, perhaps tellingly, in those days I had an air conditioner in the bedroom but not out in the living room, where the kitchen was. That doesn't mean I settled. I went to Dean & DeLuca, the pricey gourmet emporium near my office, and picked up an array of cured meats, cheeses, and a baguette for us to eat for dinner and the best Greek yogurt to eat drizzled with honey for breakfast. We were making our way through a case of white Bordeaux I had purchased earlier in the year. I didn't care what anything cost. There was no price I could put on the affection I wanted to show Marcus, and if I couldn't show it to him through my talents in the kitchen, well then, I was just going to have to go overboard in my purchases. Marcus showed me the same generosity when I went to stay with him.

Up near Columbia University, where he parked the Vespa, there was a great big wonderful market where Marcus procured a similar bounty: giant strawberries, yogurt from Vermont, organic orange juice, and good coffee. From there, we took the subway two stops up to his place. He didn't park the Vespa near his apartment because the neighborhood was too sketchy. This was tedious and took away some of the advantage of having a boyfriend with wheels, but I didn't make a fuss about it.

Nor did I wait long to ask him to remove Renee Lachaise's "I love you" from the wall (the eight-by-ten portrait of the two of them that hung in the studio came down of its own accord), and I, inspired by that missive, made the same declaration to Marcus preposterously early. He said he loved me, too.

My friends, for the most part, had no problem with the fact that Marcus was twenty years my senior. Ginia was predictably enthusiastic, as she tends to be whenever I'm dating someone who has a job. (Though I'm not sure you could call what Marcus did a job. It was hard to know how he made any money. How much could one get for a cartoon in *The New Yorker*? And his were picked up only sporadically. His fortunes depended on the flow of his ideas and the whims of the cartoon editor that particular week. But Harlem is not too expensive, I suppose.) There was a delay in the introduction, because at the time, Ginia was getting to know the man she would eventually marry and was spending most of her evenings alone with him. When Marcus and I showed up at her apartment one night when she was in the midst of one of her early dates, she was impressed by our easy manner together. I felt smug in my conviction that I had found an unconventional relationship that really seemed to suit me.

On Sunday nights, the evening before *The New Yorker*'s weekly meeting between cartoonists and their editor, I would try to help Marcus come up with captions to be placed under the pictures he drew. That's how he liked to work, image first, then words. I could never come up with anything good, as much as I wanted to help with his cash flow. Marcus took any opportunity to show up at the offices of *Harper's Magazine,* where he met many of my colleagues, most of whom remembered him from the game. He came out for drinks with me and Lewis Lapham, the magazine's editor—even this older mentor of mine seemed to approve.

Only Jennifer Romanello—a former work colleague turned close friend who serves a more sagelike role in my life on both career and romantic fronts—wasn't buying it.

"What are you going to do with *him*?" she asked.

"I don't know, love him for the rest of his life? Marry him?"

She scoffed at the idea with a half laugh, accompanied by a dismissive wave of the hand that bruised my unpractical soul. But what did she know? She got married in her twenties to a professor who had been in love with her from the time they were both in eighth grade. She couldn't possibly understand how hard love had been for me and how it might be possible that a divorced fifty-seven-year-old could be construed as a good bet in my mind. And I hadn't even told her about his last girlfriend.

Marcus and I went nearly every weekend to Connecticut, where neither my mother nor my aunt scoffed, at least not in my earshot. He really dug that place, and I couldn't quite believe how much fun I was having there with him. Marcus, once a ponytailed hippie, knew how to bake bread and wowed the older women by getting up early and baking biscuits for breakfast. We found a farmer's market over in the next town I hadn't known existed. One rare weekend when my mother stayed back in the city, I took charge of dinner. I made lamb burgers accompanied by slices of tomatoes from the farmer's

market drizzled with olive oil and sprinkled with fleur de sel along with an orzo
salad with feta cheese. We created old-
fashioned strawberry shortcakes from
the leftover biscuits, slicing them in half
and layering them with strawberries and
whipped cream. Aunt Marie, a woman
who never met a dessert she didn't like,
was sold on Marcus that evening. The
three of us had a thoroughly enjoyable
meal out on the back deck. It was the best
time I ever had with my aunt.

～～　～～　～～　～～

Lamb Burgers

1 1/2 pounds ground lamb

1/2 cup minced fresh mint

2 garlic cloves, pressed

1 tablespoon paprika

1 teaspoon salt

1/2 teaspoon cayenne pepper

1/4 teaspoon cinnamon

1 tablespoon olive oil

Combine all ingredients, shape into patties, cook on a barbecue, under the broiler, or atop the stove for 5 to 7 minutes on each side. I don't serve them with bread, I serve them with:

~~~ ~~~ ~~~ ~~~

Orzo Salad with Feta

(Adapted from *Gourmet* magazine)

   1/2 pound orzo
   Juice and zest of 1 lemon
   1/4 cup olive oil
   1/4 teaspoon salt
   Freshly ground pepper
   1/4 cup pine nuts, toasted
   3/4 cup feta, crumbled
   1/2 cup scallions, green parts only, thinly sliced

Cook the orzo according to the directions for pasta on page 32. Orzo is a quick-cooking pasta, so begin checking it at the 6-minute mark.

In a medium bowl, whisk the lemon juice, zest, olive oil, salt, and a few grindings of pepper. When the orzo is cooked, add it to the bowl and stir. Let it cool, then add the remaining ingredients. Add salt and pepper to taste.

Serves 4.

∼∼ ∼∼ ∼∼ ∼∼

Marcus's Strawberry Shortcakes

I have no idea how he made them. I'd use Bisquick.

"It looks like he's not going anywhere," I said to my mother one day when we were driving to the Stop & Shop in Connecticut, basking in this newfound feeling of security.

"It looks like you'll have to be the one to get rid of him," she said, nothing disparaging in her voice, at least not that I detected. It wasn't until after the fact that I learned she thought Marcus was full of it from the get-go. At the time, she expressed her reservations only in subtle ways, like cautioning me against going on long drives (to Connecticut, for instance) in Marcus's car. She wasn't thrilled about me riding on the back of the Vespa, either. I ignored these small pleas.

It had been a while since I'd felt that kind of hold on anyone. Marcus called constantly. He wanted to see me all the time. I was so broken by past disappointments that I needed his neediness to feel safe; thus I made myself available all the time. If he called me at work at four p.m. to say he was in the neighborhood, I would drop everything to go meet him. By five p.m., we would be drinking cold white wine in my bed. One rainy evening when the weather had cooled down enough for me to turn on the stove, I made a lovely little pasta for Marcus, spaghetti dressed only in a peignoir of truffle oil, sprinkled with parmigiano. This is a simple yet elegant dish, a luxurious and romantic supper for when all you really want to do is laze about in bed.

～～～～～～～

Spaghettini in a White Truffle Oil Peignoir

Salt
1/2 pound spaghettini (or thin spaghetti)
3 tablespoons white truffle oil
Freshly grated parmigiano
Freshly ground pepper

Cook spaghettini according to the directions for pasta on page 32. Drain and return to pot, add truffle oil. Divide into two bowls, get back in bed, bring along the cheese and pepper.

Clothing optional.

Renee Lachaise came up from time to time, as did Ethan, who was a more apt counterpart to Renee than Mitch, who had left me more flummoxed than heartbroken. And proving that no New Yorker is an absolute stranger to another, Marcus had heard Ethan's name before he met me.

Oddly, Renee had mentioned him to Marcus because a work friend of hers knew Ethan and happened to have a crush on him that she talked about incessantly. There was yet another connection between Marcus and Ethan. Marcus's son used to date Ethan's cousin Emily, whom I knew quite well; we even had dinner with her in Florence during her semester abroad. I was so amazed by all these coincidences that I couldn't resist calling Ethan and sharing them with him. Ethan knew Marcus, too, from his *New Yorker* days. He may have thought it was a little strange that I was dating someone so old, but he reserved any comment. Ethan, I learned in that conversation, had recently broken up with my successor, so I magnanimously let him know about his secret admirer, who turned out to be not so secret after all, just an old friend of Ethan's whom he had been spending a lot of time with and who was feeling a little more than he was feeling. Sound familiar?

Somewhere around week four, things with Marcus began to feel a little different.

I first noticed it while sitting with him on a rock near the water at low tide. I realized that good feeling I initially had in his presence was gone and in its place was . . . boredom. I panicked, albeit silently, and racked my brain, trying to understand what could have possibly changed. I deduced that my affection for Marcus was based on the escapist joy of seeing myself through his eyes, the eyes of someone who had no idea who I was but had instantly concluded that I was da bomb. The charge of that was so strong, it even made Connecticut seem exciting. It had been such a lovely idyll, but there, on that rock, the magic spell seemed to all of a sudden wear off.

As my feelings changed, so did Marcus's demeanor. Which came first, I really cannot say. I only know that he was no longer the happy-go-lucky biscuit baker. When my mother—still believing that Marcus's ardor was immutable—asked him to clean the leaves out of the gutters, he wasn't exactly whistling while he worked, as he had when he'd cheerfully weeded the flower beds (both in front of the house and behind it) that first weekend, the one that was the best of his life.

I refused to accept the simple probability that Marcus and I just may not have been right for each other. I wanted a relationship to work out so badly that I continued with this presumed bird in the hand, hoping that if I could just get my head right, things would be the way they were on the Fourth of July. I didn't tell anyone what I was feeling, I just let them all continue to believe that I was on cloud nine with Pops. In an attempt to understand why things were all of a sudden not working, I went with my standard explanation: There was something wrong with me. This is always a splendid fallback position, because if that is the case, there is hope that I can fix it. The discomfort will go away if I just try a little harder or make something that tastes really, really good.

Heat wave be damned, desperate times

call for desperate measures—when we got back to my place in Brooklyn, I turned on the oven and put together this parmigiana with eggplants from the Connecticut farmer's market. It was extraordinary, and Marcus managed to drum up some of that old-time over-the-top zeal, but not enough to salvage our dwindling rapport.

~~~ ~~~ ~~~ ~~~

Ineffectual Eggplant Parmigiana

- 3 large eggplants
- 1/2 cup plus 1 tablespoon olive oil
- 1 onion, chopped
- 1 teaspoon dried oregano
- 1 (28-ounce) can chopped tomatoes (or whole if you feel like pureeing them yourself with a hand blender or in a food processor; I don't)
- 1 tablespoon red wine
- 1 large pinch sugar
- 1 cup fresh basil leaves
- 1/4 cup walnuts, chopped and toasted
- 1/3 cup plain bread crumbs
- 1 teaspoon olive oil

1/2 cup freshly grated parmigiano
1 cup grated mozzarella

Preheat oven to 450 degrees.

Slice the eggplants crosswise into 1/2-inch pieces, lay on a baking sheet, and brush both sides with 1/2 cup olive oil. Bake each side for 15 minutes.

Meanwhile, heat 1 tablespoon olive oil in a large skillet over medium heat, add chopped onion, and sauté until the onion is soft (about 5 to 7 minutes). Add oregano and stir, then add tomatoes; bring to a simmer, cover, and reduce the heat to low. Cook for 20 minutes, then add wine, sugar, and basil.

While the sauce is cooking, chop walnuts and toast them in a small skillet over low heat, then add them to bread crumbs and mix them together with 1 teaspoon olive oil.

When the eggplants are browned on both sides, remove them from the oven and reduce heat to 375 degrees.

Add a little of the sauce to the bottom

of a 9 by 9-inch baking dish (or whatever baking dish you have that will accommodate the eggplant and most of
the sauce), then sprinkle a little parmigiano on top. Add a layer of eggplant
followed by sauce, a sprinking of mozzarella, a sprinkling of parmigiano, and
continue until all the eggplant is used
up. Cover the top with the bread crumb—
walnut mixture and bake until browned
and bubbling, about 35 to 40 minutes.

Serves the 2 of you, plus the 3 other
people you wish were there to help keep
the conversation going.

The next weekend, we stayed in the city.
Those two days stretched before me like
an aeon. How would I make it through?
Friday night we went with his son to see
the Jicks play in Prospect Park. The rain
was pouring down, and we shielded ourselves from it with newspapers we found
in the trash, though we should have just
left since neither father nor son knew who

Stephen Malkmus was. Saturday was a stunning day, but I felt trapped, not that it occurred to me to try to get away. I didn't want to hurt Marcus's feelings, and I didn't know what I would do by myself anyway. It was not the first or, sadly, the last time I have found myself stricken with Stockholm syndrome.

We went to Central Park and ate ice-cream bars; that took about two hours. Then it was one-thirty, a long time until dinner. I was living from meal to meal; at least at mealtime there was something to do, and better yet, something to drink. We took the long way back to Brooklyn on the Vespa, going over the 59th Street Bridge, cruising through Long Island City, Williamsburg, and Fort Greene; then I suggested we go for a spin around Red Hook and take in some of the extraordinary views of the harbor and Statue of Liberty. This was a good idea except for the fact that that's where the Vespa ran over something that gave it a flat tire. Now I was stuck with Marcus walking the Vespa through the middle of nowhere, looking for a place to get it repaired. We weren't far from my brother Matthew's apartment, so we went there and Matthew helped Marcus park the scooter. We were stuck, Vespaless in Brooklyn, with two long hours until dinner.

While we were sitting around my brother's apartment waiting for a reasonable dining hour to arrive, Matthew mentioned that one of our Italian cousins had written looking for a place some friends of hers could stay when they visited New York. I wasn't inclined to give up my apartment, but Marcus insisted I stay with him and let them have my place for the week. What a kind and generous soul. I should have been happy with him. Why wasn't I?

Marcus took charge of the entertainment committee when Sonia and Andrea arrived. He was thrilled to hang out with real Italians and for his daughter to polish her rusty language skills. He took them to a *New Yorker* softball game in Central Park, he arranged dinners at ethnic restaurants in pockets of New York far from the tourist beat. His efforts did prop up my mood a little bit. Sonia and Andrea were superimpressed. They thought we were a fantastic couple, and through their eyes I could once again see us that way, too.

When they left, Marcus became somewhat elusive. He no longer called to announce his every move; now he was AWOL for long stretches of time. His carefree middle-aged artist-about-town attitude was all but gone. A parking ticket, which he would have shrugged off in our early days, sent him into a lather. We were still going to Connecticut every weekend, but Marcus no longer wanted to hear my music, once so fresh, on the drive up there. Instead, we listened to his bluesy backroom bar mixes. The sort of stuff my sister Carla's bad-boy boyfriends used to listen to in the seventies when they came over and hung out in our rec room and used my doll carriage as an ashtray. I didn't like those guys, and I didn't like their music. The memory did

not do much for my endeavor to resuscitate an attraction to Marcus.

One night when we were in bed at his
apartment, the buzzer on the intercom
rang. Marcus ignored it. It rang and rang.
Then there was a knock on the apartment door. Marcus went to it, then came
back and told me it was some crackhead
woman looking for a guy named Paco.

"I told her Paco didn't live here."

The next morning, I got up well before Marcus and went to the kitchen to
make coffee. Gone was the nice French
roast he used to buy; in its place was
some cheap Café Bustelo, the kind of coffee you get in a bodega. I used to drink it
back in my starving publishing assistant
days. I set up Marcus's espresso pot, but
something went wrong and wet coffee
grinds ricocheted all over the kitchen. I
was frantically trying to wipe down the
kitchen with a moldy sponge, dying for
coffee, and wondering why Marcus, who
used to spring out of bed at the crack of
dawn, wasn't yet awake. There was no

coffee, no orange juice, and nothing to eat. When Marcus finally emerged and I left for work, he didn't wait with me for the elevator as he usually did; he just left me standing there alone.

Then he announced that he would be spending the next week at his family's lake house up in Canada for his annual vacation with his children and ex-wife. "I would invite you, but . . ." I understood. In any case, I had no desire to go on vacation with him and his ex-wife and children. Marcus wanted to leave the Vespa parked in the small yard in front of my house while he was away. On the Friday before he left for his trip, we had tickets to see the Brooklyn Cyclones, a local minor league baseball team that he really wanted to see. I had not heard from him all day. I spent the afternoon with Kit at a tag sale, waiting for Marcus to call, and while Kit was helping me lug home a painting, we found him on my stoop, waiting. The painting, a Watteau reproduction, inspired one more burst of faux mensch from Marcus, who offered to paint over some of the spots on the canvas that were chipped. He was tough to read; he looked sullen on the stoop, but then he morphed into the good guy, always willing to help, especially with art.

But as we rode out to Coney Island on the Vespa, my hands felt wrong wrapped around Marcus's waist, and he wasn't saying much. Alarmed by the prices at the concession stand, he got us one beer and one popcorn to share. Not long after we took our seats in the bleachers, I noticed that the beer had moved from its initial spot between us to Marcus's right, where I couldn't get at it. He wasn't concerned with my need for alcohol or the players on the field. Not even the man dressed as a giant baseball, who danced around the aisles in between innings, could evoke any sort of reaction from him. At the seventh-inning stretch, there was a fireworks display on the beach. Marcus didn't even look. "This is kind of boring," he said, and with that we left.

Marcus parked the Vespa in front of my house and took the subway home. He was off to Canada the next morning.

"I'll call you when I get there," he said as he left. "I guess I'll have to since you never call me."

What was that about? I couldn't understand what it was or where it came from, but I could also no longer deny that something was very wrong. I had been having doubts about Marcus for weeks, but surely that was just me putting up roadblocks where there weren't any. I didn't have any hard evidence to explain my lack of satisfaction besides maybe an unwillingness to clean gutters here or phoning a few hours late there. I was a pro at ignoring those and working on my own thing. I was going to get better, then he'd get better and we would be happy again, just as we were for that first five or so minutes of what should merely have been a fun, inappropriate summer fling.

I couldn't bear another story gone wrong,

no matter how wrong that story was. I spent Saturday sick with worry over what could have happened. Marcus's original demeanor was a memory, but he never behaved with hostility the way he had that previous evening. And though he wasn't making me happy, I didn't want to lose him. My family knew him and (as far as I could tell) liked him, Ginia was rooting for us, and most of my work friends and colleagues had witnessed our meeting, and those who hadn't had met him when I paraded him around the office on his many visits.

The weekend was cloudy, and I was trapped in that mental prison known as waiting-for-the-phone-to-ring. I checked my cell phone every two minutes. Saturday night, I called him. He had groused about my never calling, after all. I got only his voice mail. Sunday morning, I went to Mass to try to get some peace, but nothing worked. I scratched and scratched at a mosquito bite I probably got at that silly game.

I spent Monday in a state of extreme

stress. I dined with my brother Matthew and his wife, Elizabeth, on Tuesday, and they brushed off my worries. They adored Marcus and were convinced that some logical explanation of his silence would emerge when he did.

On Wednesday at lunch, I went to a lingerie sample sale, even though I thought that might be bad luck in light of what was going on. Still, I bought some lacy underpinnings. Not long after I returned to work, an e-mail arrived from Marcus.

G.
Two things:
You've obviously been talking to some-one a lot about me.
I've run off with Renee Lachaise. I'm as madly in love with her as I was the night we met.
M.

My heart was palpitating. I grabbed the phone and called Marcus, but there was no answer on his home phone or cell. (As if someone that cowardly would answer his phone, but I wasn't thinking straight.) "You can't break up with me like that," I said in my messages. I didn't know what the hell he was talking about. *You've obviously been talking to someone a lot about me.*

Not only was this nonsensical, it was angry, and there was nothing between us to warrant that. Good that he was gone, but was the kick in the face really necessary?

For whatever reason, I needed to make some sense out of that e-mail. Okay, he "ran off with Renee Lachaise," that was clear. But the "talking about" him was sheer lunacy, and yet, I must speak lunatic because I was able to trace the meaning of it with a call to Ethan. Barring that, I could at least find a way to blame myself for what happened.

"Did you tell Erin O'Brien that I was dating Marcus Caldwell?" Erin was that friend of Renee's who had the crush on Ethan, and he had every right to tell her if he wanted to, that wasn't the issue, it's just that if Ethan had told Erin, then my lunatic dictionary could translate the missive into something like "If you hadn't told Ethan, it wouldn't have gotten back to Renee." The whole thing was madness, and I should have been thanking the Lord that psychopath was out of my life, but instead I actually spent a couple of days regretting that I had ever said anything to Ethan.

"He's fifty-seven years old, he should get some balls," said John Mallon, an old friend I'd always had a little crush on whom I happened to have drinks scheduled with that evening. His funny comments about the episode had me roaring, and the Bellinis we were drinking brought out the two specks of flirt left in me. I ended up dragging him back to my apartment just to put a better spin on a horrible day. To borrow from the *Sex and the City* episode in which Carrie gets arrested for smoking pot the day Berger breaks up with her on a Post-it note: I wanted to turn it into the day I made out with John Mallon rather than the day I got dumped by an AARP member with a psychotic e-mail. It helped to have John with me when I got home to find the Vespa gone and the same demented text on a handwritten note slipped under my door.

"Even his language dates him!" said my wise friend Jennifer, mercifully sparing me any "I told you so's" when I told her about the note. "Who says they've 'run off' with someone in this day and age?"

"You'll hear from him again," said Ginia. "Not before Columbus Day and not after Christmas." She was right about hearing from him again, but wrong about the timing. His attempt to woo me back commenced a few days shy of Columbus Day and continued until Christmas.

He called, he sent notes, he had cupcakes delivered to my office. They were pretty; one was yellow with a little bee on it, the other was white with pink flowers drawn in icing. But even I wouldn't eat them. Not wanting to waste food, even from him, I tried to pawn them off on my colleagues at *Harper's,* but they, in solidarity, wouldn't eat them, either. They ended up in the garbage. I ignored all of his attempts. I had as much interest in seeing Marcus again as I would in hanging out with Jeffrey Dahmer.

The nice-guy shtick must have taken tremendous energy for Marcus to keep up, especially at his age. That exertion must have been what kept him so trim and not surreptitious hours spent at the gym every day while I was at work, as I originally suspected.

I exorcised him from my life by making some cupcakes of my own.

~~~ ~~~ ~~~ ~~~

Fuck-You Cakes

For the cupcakes (yellow cake, of course):
Cupcake liners
2 cups cake flour
2 teaspoons baking powder
1/2 teaspoon salt
1 stick (1/2 cup) butter, softened
1 cup sugar
3 large eggs, room temperature
1 1/2 teaspoons vanilla
3/4 cup whole milk

Preheat oven to 350 degrees.

Insert liners into muffin tins. Sift together flour, baking powder, and salt and set aside. Cream butter and sugar with a hand mixer (or a standing mixer fitted with a paddle) at medium speed until fluffy; add eggs one at time, then the vanilla, and beat until smooth. Reduce mixer speed to low and add the sifted ingredients to the butter mixture a little at a time, alternating with the milk until fully incorporated. Do not overmix, as this will make for tough cupcakes and you've suffered enough.

Spoon batter into muffin tins, filling each one a third of the way. Bake until tops are golden and springy, 20 to 25 minutes.

Yield: About 12.

～～ ～～ ～～ ～～

Chocolate Bourbon Frosting

(Because you need a drink)

1/4 cup unsweetened cocoa
2 to 3 tablespoons bourbon (depending on how bad it was)

4 tablespoons milk
1 stick unsalted butter, very soft
1 box confectioners' sugar
1 to 2 tablespoons milk

In a small bowl, whisk the cocoa, bourbon, and 2 tablespoons milk. Cream the butter with a hand mixer or stand-up mixer at medium speed until smooth, then add the sugar 1 cup at a time until fully incorporated. Add the bourbon mixture and continue beating until the color is uniform, then the additional milk a little at a time until the frosting is fluffy and spreadable.

Don't be so angry with yourself that you eat more than one or two cupcakes. Be angry with him! Bring whatever is left to work. Your colleagues will eat these and you'll feel lighter for having shed him and not OD'ing on cupcakes.

From Sex and the City to Nun

The Marcus episode scarred me. In fact, with all due respect to Saint Francis, I felt as though I had been marked with the stigmata of bad experiences. I was embarrassed at the office because everyone knew about Marcus, and now (through my own reportage) everyone knew he was gone. Certainly no one cared one way or the other, but we can't help believing that people are way more focused on our lives than they actually are. I winced at the memory of parading him around the office, so proud of the wrinkly-scaled catch I had brought home from the softball game, and how the whole thing played itself out before everyone's eyes.

I didn't have to impose a moratorium on dating this time: I was left with post-traumatic stress disorder and was much too damaged to consider it. Even the men who were my friends bothered me. My solution was to seek attention just from those I knew were truly off-limits: "The only men I want to be friends with are gay men, married men, or priests," I declared to Ginia. The jokes were too easy—she refrained from making any. And she agreed that there were a lot of ex-boyfriends and boys whose connection to me was ambiguous hanging around: Kit was living down the block with a woman he would eventually marry and divorce; Henry, the author I had once kissed and who had fixed me up with Mitch, lived around the corner and would come over every Saturday morning for coffee and toast; even Ethan's familiar address would appear at the top of my e-mail inbox from time to time. All these men who couldn't or wouldn't give me what I was looking for were taking up space in my life. Following tenets more New Age than Christian, I got rid of them all in order to free that space for new things.

So I turned to the church I had discovered just before Marcus knocked me off track, and I dated Father Joel, albeit in an utterly chaste and Vatican-sanctioned way.

Joel is a priest who was, at that time, in his early thirties. He studied at Oxford and is proficient in Latin and ancient Greek, not that that would affect my dialogue with him in any way, but it pleases me to know people who are accomplished. Joel wears little round silver glasses, and he looks as if he stepped out of *Brideshead Revisited* (the PBS miniseries, not the film). I met him at a new members dinner, where I confessed to him that I had not gone to confession for twenty-eight years. I joked that I was tempted to give the sacrament another go, but only if cocktails were involved. Joel promised Manhattans if I told him my sins, and he kept his word—only we imbibed them not in the confessional, but at a nearby bar, where we smoked and drank and got a little too tipsy. From then on we stuck to red wine, which we drank regularly at Bacchus, a bistro equidistant from my apartment and the church, whose French owners had a lax attitude about the city's smoking laws. Joel and I sat for hours after dinner, drinking coffee, smoking, and talking. Joel fantasized about doing missionary work at the restaurant, bringing the French staff back into the faith. "Ah, France, the first daughter of the church," he'd say with a sigh. He would convert them one espresso at a time.

I always wanted to be friends with a priest. The vocation, to me, seems more alternative than anything the modern world can come up with. There's nothing quite as out there as giving it all up (or most of it) for God.

As you may have surmised, the church I go to isn't the dreary parish that many, including me, associate with Catholic churches. It is tastefully decorated, the choir is world class, and Sunday Masses are packed with people who aren't just making grocery lists in their heads or killing time before the big game. There are four priests, each one terribly attractive in his own way: Joel, with his dry wit and sharp intellect; Mark, a handsome Australian in his early fifties, who is more heartfelt; Dennis, whose style is a little pop psyche, which I'm all for; and Anthony, who just entered the priesthood and is full of earnest goodwill and insight. Every Sunday, one of them offers an illuminating perspective on the faith, and most times it manages to coincide with whatever is on my mind that week. It's a great respite from city life. On the best days, I can get lost in meditation (rare, but it does happen). I've been in and out of church all my life, but when I found this place, I knew I was staying. To anyone who would listen, I berated myself for not finding it sooner. "You found us when you were ready to find us," was

Joel's reassuring reply. Maybe. Maybe I'll find that other thing when I'm ready, too. Maybe I'm not as ready as I think I am. Still, I was having my most satisfying love affair in recent memory with that church. I couldn't stop talking about it. I told every Catholic I knew who went to church (a small number) and tried to reinvigorate a few who fell away.

Besides Sister Mary Virginia, who once locked me in a closet in second grade and told me she was going to leave me there all weekend, my memories of Catholic school are good. From first to eighth grade, I was educated by cloistered nuns who wore habits. Sister Aimee, my first-grade teacher, was a classic example of what the life of the spirit can do for you, best-case scenario. She was smiling, beatific, wise. Her fingernails were bitten to the quick, but let's not hang that on celibacy; with all my sexual freedom, I too am an incurable nail biter. My high school nuns were more worldly; they wore civilian clothes and were passionately political—their main concern was the situation in Nicaragua; they played guitar and sang songs in praise of the Sandinistas. We fasted for Oxfam, then spent the evening in the monastery making soup and baking bread. The school offered classes in existentialism; we read Samuel Beckett, Franz Kafka, and Albert Camus.

The church gave me a progressive education, as it banished the occasional loneliness of my childhood. That's why I keep going back, even though I am a slave to carnality and probably have no right to be there.

Fed up with just about every man except Jesus (and even he confounded me), and without any seriousness of intent, I imagined becoming a nun. Usually, though, my daydreams tended to view this calling as a temporary position: I would enter a convent and write a memoir entitled *From Sex and the City to Nun*, and it would be a huge best seller. Naturally, it would end with me falling in love with a handsome young priest and both of us shaking off our holy orders. No, I just couldn't give up hope of finding forever love. Call it faith, if you will, I just can't lose it.

Still, I was in no way at peace with my lot. I couldn't conceive of why God would bless me with such well-honed domestic skills, then deny me a family to share them with. I was in my late thirties, I wanted to have a real home with a real kitchen where my husband and I would host my brothers and sisters, nieces and nephews, for holidays. I was stuck, living in the same apartment I'd moved into with Kit almost fifteen years earlier, with the same tiny kitchen. Then, like a good Catholic, I said, "Fuck it. I'll accept my life as it is." I would host Easter in the apartment I had, however imperfect the setting or situation. If this is what God gave me, I would operate within His parameters.

Lent was a breeze. I abstained from sex. Which was a joke because even if Catholics were permitted to have sex on any day of the year before marriage, there was not a soul on God's earth who wanted to have sex with me. But that was okay; the enlightened nuns who educated me always said it was better to do something good for others than give up some silly thing like chocolate for Lent, which didn't do anything to make the world a better place. I would cook Easter dinner for my family, I would be cheerful about my life, and my positive spirit would reverberate clear to the Middle East.

Kit came over and helped me move my farmhouse table from its little niche to the center of the living room after I apologized for being out of touch. (He's used to me being a freak—in fact, "freak" is practically his nickname for me—and he always forgives.) I bought an additional table from the Salvation Army and put them together to make one long table that transformed the bulk of my living space into a giant dining room. I spent weeks planning the menu, settling on a first course of homemade gnocchi with a simple sauce of tomato and butter, followed by the requisite leg of lamb. I made the gnocchi the weekend before and froze them, then spent every evening of Holy Week transporting supplies to my apartment. I loved opening the freezer and looking at the gnocchi tucked away in Ziploc bags; their shape, formed with a fork and my thumb, was absolutely perfect. I attended services for Holy Thursday and Good Friday. Saturday I bought lilies and tulips and daffodils. I couldn't help but feel the joy that reflecting upon Jesus's death and resurrection is supposed to make you feel, which you may have to be educated by nuns to fathom.

~~~ ~~~ ~~~ ~~~

No Nookie Gnocchi

For the gnocchi:

> **2 russet potatoes**
> **1 egg**
> **1 teaspoon salt**
> **Pinch freshly grated nutmeg**
> **1 heaping cup flour, plus extra flour for dusting**
> **Salt**

Freshly grated parmigiano
Freshly grated pepper

Put the potatoes in a pot with enough water to cover, bring to a boil, and cook, partially covered, until they are just tender, 35 to 40 minutes. Remove the potatoes to a cutting board and peel with a paring knife as soon as you can stand to touch them, then run them through a potato ricer or food mill, spreading them out on a cutting board to cool completely.

Mix the egg, salt, and nutmeg. Form the cooled potatoes into a mound and pour the egg mixture into it. Begin kneading the potato and egg mixture with your hands, adding the flour a little at a time, being careful not to overwork the dough.

When the flour is evenly combined with the potato and the dough is only a little sticky, divide it into 4 pieces. Roll each piece into a long, narrow tube like a garden snake and slice it crosswise into soft little pillows, each 1/2 inch wide. Rest each pillow on the tip of your thumb and impress it with the tines of a fork lightly dusted with flour, creating a ribbed surface for the sauce to cling to. Keep a bowl of flour nearby to dip the fork into, as it will become tacky—or better yet, keep some extra forks nearby.

Add the gnocchi about 10 at a time to a pot of salted boiling water. When they rise to the top, they're done. Remove them to a serving bowl with a slotted spoon or spider and continue to cook in batches. Toss with the sauce and serve with grated parmigiano and freshly grated pepper.

Yield: About 6 dozen.

For the sauce:

(Adapted from Marcella Hazan's *Essentials of Classic Italian Cooking*)

1 (28-ounce) can whole tomatoes
1/2 cup (1 stick) butter
1 medium onion, peeled and cut in half
1 tablespoon sugar
1/4 cup red wine
1 teaspoon salt

Put all ingredients in a large saucepan
over medium heat, bring to a simmer,
then lower heat and cook for 45 minutes,
stirring occasionally. Remove onion before tossing sauce with the gnocchi.

Over this period of celibacy, I became
a cooking slut; I would do it wherever
and whenever anyone would let me. I vol-
unteered to be the chef for parish coun-
cil meetings and member get-togethers
at church. When my friends Lucinda and
John had their first baby, I went over to
their house and made spaghetti and meatballs for the exhausted new parents.

The benefits to them here were obvious: a home-cooked meal, an extra pair
of hands, adult conversation. The benefit for me was time with their baby.
Oddly, I find that time with other people's children thoroughly fulfills my
maternal desires. I'm not overly concerned with bearing a child, and the
fact is that I most likely never will. With-

out a stable relationship, I can't even fathom the idea—to me it's like worrying about where you're going to put all that money before you even scratch the lottery ticket (and romance, to me, seems about as precarious as winning the lottery). Children were definitely included in the life I pictured with Ethan, but when I lost Ethan, it wasn't the prospect of children that I felt was brutally torn from me, it was the prospect of a life with *him*. If I find another man to love, I may want to have his babies, but I know it's probably too late. Somehow this scenario doesn't haunt me. I can't say how I'll feel ten years from now, but for the present I consider being spared that regret a tremendous, albeit unexplainable, gift. In the future, should the desire seize me, I'll consider science or adoption.

My visits to John and Lucinda have become regular monthly events, and no matter how many creative suggestions I come up with for other dishes, they always insist on the meatballs. I don't mind. I can make them with my eyes closed.

～～～ ～～ ～～～

Spaghetti and Meatballs for Cooking Sluts and Those Who Love Them

For meatballs:

- 1 pound chopped beef (I like to use chuck, but Lucinda prefers a leaner cut; either way, they're delicious)
- 3/4 cup plain bread crumbs
- 1 clove garlic, minced
- 1/4 cup freshly grated parmigiano
- 2 eggs
- 1/4 cup milk
- 1 teaspoon salt
- 1/4 teaspoon freshly ground pepper
- 1/2 cup chopped Italian parsley
- 2 tablespoons olive oil, plus 2 more tablespoons reserved for browning

Throw all the above ingredients in a large bowl and blend well with your hands. Shape into balls (you choose the size).

In a large skillet, heat the reserved 2 tablespoons olive oil and sauté the meatballs until they are browned on all sides. Remove to plate lined with two paper towels. Set aside.

Yield: About 20 (1-inch-diameter) meatballs.

For sauce:

2 tablespoons olive oil
Big pinch hot red pepper flakes (optional)
1 (28-ounce) can chopped or whole (the better choice) tomatoes from Italy
1 tablespoon tomato paste
1/4 cup red wine
2 teaspoons sugar
2 teaspoons salt
1 pound spaghetti
1/4 cup packed basil leaves
Freshly grated parmigiano for passing at the table

Heat the olive oil in a large sauté pan over medium heat, then add the pepper flakes (if using), tomatoes (and their juices, breaking them up with your hands, if using whole), and tomato paste. Add wine, sugar, salt, and meatballs. Bring to a simmer, then lower heat to medium-low; cook, stirring often, for 40 minutes.

Cook spaghetti according to the directions for pasta on page 32. Drain and return to pot, then add a few ladlefuls of sauce and a few leaves of basil torn with your hands. Add pasta to individual bowls garnished with 1 to 2 meatballs (depending on the appetites of your friends) and a few torn basil leaves. Pass parmigiano at table.

Serves 4 to 6.

Single-Girl Suppers

If a tree falls in the woods and no one hears it, does it make a sound? If I make a splendid rigatoni with sausages, broccoli, onions, and butter, and only I taste it, did it exist?

I've spent just as much time single as I have as half of a couple, and though I much prefer cooking for two to cooking for one, if one is all I have, I cook for her. It's not like I only got into this racket to please men, though I do get a thrill out of feeding those unfathomable creatures. Many have found succor on that old green sofa, where sooner or later I'm going to offer them a cookie, but never enough to sign up for a lifetime of three well-made squares cheerfully provided daily. I don't blame any of them for my situation (well, I sort of do but not fully, at least); my logical mind knows that in every case I got precisely what I was looking for. I'm where I am because of me. I haven't gotten to the bottom of why that is, but I have a battery of professionals working with me on the case.

Because cooking and eating well are my raison d'être, I don't stop when there's no one else to feed. Even if it's just me, I make breakfasts of pancakes and sausages or French toast, just as I would if I'd woken up with a man in my bed. The idea of going to the café on the corner for coffee seems insane to me. I'll make myself a Niçoise salad with olives, capers, red onion, grape tomatoes, parsley, and canned Italian tuna for lunch. At dinner I'll roast some fish, grill a steak, or invent a pasta from whatever happens to be in the fridge. Those dishes, born out of random couplings dictated by whatever is available, are the ones that make me saddest. They are never to be duplicated; I am the only one who will ever know how delicious they were. I'm conflicted about whether that is good enough, just as I'm conflicted about whether it's better to be with someone or to be alone.

There are many things I like about being by myself and few people who can provide me with the sort of peace I get buzzing around my apartment, singing along to Belle & Sebastian's "Funny Little Frog" as it emerges from speakers planted wirelessly in every room of my apartment—including the kitchen, of course—a system I masterminded and installed all on my own.

I manage to be both ashamed and proud of how self-sufficient I am. When I was going to an office every day, I hesitated to admit to colleagues that I couldn't wait to go straight home after work, roast myself a piece of salmon over a bed of asparagus (450-degree oven, handful of asparagus drizzled with olive oil, a sprinkle of salt, and a grinding of pepper, salmon fillet over it seasoned in same manner, roast for twenty minutes, squeeze a little lemon on top, and chop an herb and stick it on there if you wish, but delicious even without), and sit with it and a glass of cool white wine at my dining room table *toute seule*. Back then I found this vastly preferable to postwork socializing at a bar. I love drinking, but only when there's food involved. When I had to go, I was the one showing up with a bag of pretzels.

There are as many pros to being alone as there are cons to being coupled. Sacrifices you must make to be in a couple that you don't have to make when you are single, and many pleasures to being alone that you forfeit when you are bound to another person. Like being able to watch whatever you want on TV—my current fave is *Gossip Girl;* I don't think any man would abide that habit (well, Mitch might, but I won't give him the chance to find out). When you're with a man, you have to pretend you like shows like *The Wire,* which I can't believe any woman actually likes, though my married friends swear up and down that they truly, truly do (and I'll take them at their word, but you won't find me watching it). Or being able to jet off to Cannes with a friend who is going there on business, as I recently did, without having to take anyone else into consideration. Then there's having the entire bed to spread out in all by yourself.

It's the sheets that get to me—there is absolutely no way on earth to do a proper job of folding them alone. And that stuff that's fun to do in them, you really do need to be in a couple to get the most out of that. Meals, of course, are vastly more enjoyable when shared. I can't marvel about how perfect the rigatoni is to myself, though I sometimes do. Yes, as much as I like my freedom, I am convinced that it's better to be with someone than not. If nothing else, it makes it that much easier to explain yourself at group functions.

My own dinner parties are full of couples. What choice do I have? When you are my age, the lepers who remain single are few and far between. And as my guests compliment my cooking, which feels great, I also have to hear them wonder aloud how it could be that I'm not married, which feels awful. The person who brings it up is usually a man, a man married to a woman who doesn't cook. I end up wishing I were a fat, terrible cook; that way my life would make sense to me. But my reasoning is faulty. Fat people get married, and women who can't cook get married to nice men who cook for them. In fact, both of my brothers do most of the cooking for their wives, and they are quite talented. What I like most about cooking for the priests is that they never ask me why I'm not married. I don't ask them, either, but if I did, they would have canon law to explain their situation. There's nothing to explain me.

It can be lonely to be alone. But there is nothing that screams "loneliness" louder than takeout. I don't want my dinner for one brought to me by a man on a bike.

I can't stand waiting around for him to arrive. I'd rather be busy in the kitchen, not sitting around waiting for the doorbell to be rung by a man with whom I have merely a business relationship worrying about how much to tip. No, it is infinitely better to prepare your own food. I believe in a well-stocked pantry and the sense of tranquillity that comes from a well-appointed domestic life, even if it's only for me, as sad as that may sound.

Those who don't cook think it's too much trouble, especially if it's just for one. If there is anything I want to convince the world of, it is that this is not the case: Cooking is impossibly easy. Food that is prepared simply from a few fresh ingredients is the food I like best. Like this spaghetti with arugula, which involves absolutely no work if you buy baby arugula that is already washed and ready to go. I try to have some in my refrigerator at all times so I can throw together this wonderful pasta at a moment's notice.

～～～～～～～

Spaghetti with Arugula and Pine Nuts

(Adapted from *Bon Appétit* magazine)

2 to 3 ounces spaghetti (depending on how hungry you are)

1 tablespoon olive oil, plus a touch more for taste

2 heaping cups arugula (preferably prewashed baby arugula, for your sake; regular arugula is very dirty, and that's more work than you want to do right now)

1 tablespoon fresh lemon juice

Freshly ground pepper

Salt

Freshly grated parmigiano, as much as you like

1 tablespoon pine nuts, toasted

Cook the pasta according to the directions on page 32.

When the spaghetti is nearly cooked, heat the olive oil in a medium skillet over low heat, add arugula, and cook until just wilted. When the spaghetti is done, drain and add it to the arugula. Add a touch of olive oil, lemon juice, and some pepper; taste for salt, then remove from heat, add cheese and pine nuts, and serve.

Serves 1.

If you want to double this recipe and make it for a boyfriend, that's your problem.

I will allow that there could be something in my DNA that makes cooking easy for me when it is not so for other people. Those people, on the other hand, are probably gifted with a gene that makes men want to marry them, or at least ask them out on a second date. In the past few years, even this has proven a feat akin to making a soufflé that never falls. Would I trade with them? Probably.

While I've struggled with relationships, cooking has been a fairly consistent source of satisfaction. How to behave with men, I just don't have a feel for it. It doesn't come naturally to me the way creating a perfect base for any sauce does. "And then she never heard from him again," is how I'd jokingly wrap up any report of a promising date, phone conversation, or e-mail exchange. It was my defense, so that when it happened I would be protected by the fact that I expected it. I really didn't think I would never hear again. But date after date after witty banter and comic repartee, I didn't. I was astounded by the fact that I did not manage to arouse even the slightest curiosity in the criminal defense attorney, money manager, business magazine writer, book editor, or pickle maker I went out with. (The pickler actually decided he'd had enough of me while the date was still going on. He invited me back to his apartment to make me a salad. We sat on the couch and he fell asleep straight away. No steam and, worse, no salad.)

I renounced my vow of celibacy for nothing. Joel once told me that one can regain her canonical virginity after three years. I didn't want that; it took me long enough to lose my regular one in the first place.

Then, in classic New York style, I found just the thing to take my mind off all of it: real estate. I had been waiting for a man to swoop in and take me into our new home and life, but he never came and there were things I wanted to do, like cook in a real kitchen and entertain like a grown-up. I couldn't wait any longer. I had to go it alone, and in order to do that, I needed a better apartment. What did I discover? Real estate affords a girl just as much heartbreak as dating. This I took to be both disturbing and refreshing. It was nice to know there were other things in the world that had the same power over me that men had.

Was it the bridal magazines strewn about the place, whispering, *If you buy this apartment, this will happen to you, too?* that made me fall so hard for the first apartment I ever looked at? It was a condo on an up-and-coming strip of Brooklyn waterfront. Good move on the owner's part. But it was more than that. Mainly it was the kitchen with its brand-new de rigueur stainless-steel appliances: the Viking stove, the Sub-Zero refrigerator, the Bosch dishwasher. These things were even more my birthright than the white dresses in those magazines.

I lost three nights of sleep trying to figure out a formula to determine what I should offer. I jumped out of bed hourly and ran to my computer, typing in numbers: square footage, times the number of burners on the stove, divided by the prime rate, minus the balance of my savings account, divided by the number of shelves in the refrigerator. I had no idea how to figure it out, so I came up with some number that was bigger than the one they were asking for and faxed in the paperwork. Then I roasted a chicken and thought about what a better experience that would be in my new kitchen.

~~~ ~~~ ~~~ ~~~

Real Estate Roast Chicken

1 (3- to 4-pound) chicken
2 tablespoons soft butter
Salt
Freshly ground pepper
1 lemon
3 garlic cloves, peeled and crushed

Preheat oven to 375 degrees.

Rub the chicken with butter, season generously with salt and pepper, squeeze the juice of the lemon over it, and stuff the cavity with the lemon rinds and garlic. Place on a rack breast side down in a roasting pan; roast for 30 minutes, then turn breast side up, baste with pan juices, and roast for another 20 to 30 minutes, until the breast is golden and the juices that run from a pierced thigh are clear.

Yield: 2 servings.

Getting the call from the listing agent telling me that my bid didn't cut it felt just like getting dumped. I had rebuilt my life around this apartment, and then one miscalculation, and one phone call, and it was gone.

After that first taste, I got addicted to the hunt. Every Saturday I would scan *The New York Times* real estate pages and Internet to set my course for Sunday afternoon open houses. For eight months, I never saw a thing to compare with that first place. After eight months, I decided I was never going to find an apartment, so I started fixing up the one I had. I was cruising through my savings buying furniture and cookware while halfheartedly stopping by the occasional open house.

Of course, that "when you give up on it you find it" dictum was going to work for me somewhere. Unfortunately, it happened to be with real estate.

On a Saturday in February, I spotted an apartment that looked pretty nice on the Internet, but big deal, that had happened a million times. Still, I decided to go to the open house that had been scheduled for the following day.

That day coincided with a massive blizzard. I called my brother Nick, who doubled as my real estate coach.

"There can't possibly be any open houses today."

"But that's exactly when you have to go, you'll have an edge."

I called the Realtor. Were they still having an open house on Lincoln Place?

Yes, they were.

It continued to snow, hard. I called the Realtor again.

Yes, the open house was still on.

I trudged the mile and a half from my apartment in a foot of snow. Nick and his wife, Yuki, met me there. The Realtor was taking off her boots when we arrived. We lined ours up beside hers and entered. Immediately I sensed it—something felt right about this place; it wasn't perfect, but it had everything I wanted. I'd heard this was how you're supposed to feel about the man you marry, but lacking that, I'd take the apartment. Once inside, I found a nice big central foyer, which connected all the rooms. The art deco bathroom was tiled in black and white with toile de Jouy wallpaper, the large living room had French doors and ample room for dining and lounging, the bedroom had windows that looked onto a pretty courtyard. The pièce de résistance was the kitchen, which, though not enormous, was beautifully done. After a year of looking, those stainless-steel appliances, which I liked so much at first, began to seem soulless once I noticed them in every newly built condo or recently renovated co-op in New York. This kitchen had the top-of-the-line stuff, but here it was interpreted in a traditional style. There were white wooden cabinets with carved details against a backsplash of white tile with an impressed floral molding. The cabinetry continued on the doors of the refrigerator and dishwasher. There were big drawers and sliding shelves to conveniently store cookware, a microwave oven concealed behind a sliding door, a shelf for cookbooks over the sink. The woman who lived here (who was selling it because she was getting married to a German she met on Match.com) had painstakingly restored every inch of that apartment and overseen the kitchen renovation, thinking through every detail. And this single woman would be the one to enjoy it. I told the Realtor I would make an offer. I was pretty sure no one besides me would be showing up today and it would be mine.

"More people may come," she said. "I got two calls asking about the open house."

"They were both from me," I said, laughing.

I got the apartment. The roast chicken I made in my new oven was divine.

Lachlan Martyn Was Passionate ... About Food

I used any excuse to stay home from work in the first few months after moving. Furniture deliveries, the cable guy, the dishwasher repairman—all were reasons to take off an entire day. I was in love with my apartment, which only exacerbated my conflict about having a man around. Now it wasn't just my sanity that needed protecting, I had a home to guard—a feminine paradise complete with a crystal chandelier in the foyer (a relic from the house I grew up in) and a mirrored vanity table in the bedroom (a new purchase)—that didn't need mucking up with guy stuff like guitars and electronics. I distracted myself from any inklings of loneliness I might have felt by dedicating myself to adorning the place with art and eclectic furnishings. When there's something to buy, there is nothing bad to feel, and thanks to the Internet, I was buying at all hours. Packages arrived in the mail or on trucks every day. I collected paintings and photographs from flea markets or friends and spared no expense in framing them—this also had something to do with the fact that I had a crush on my framer, which was about as much of a relationship as I wanted at the time.

It was the anticipation of pain that kept me home from work the day I met Lachlan. There would be a needle full of Novocain, extensive drilling, and an hour in the chair. But when it was all over, I felt fine, and since it was a cloudless, not too warm August day, I opted for the long walk from the dentist in my old neighborhood to my new neighborhood, stopping off at Sahadi, a Brooklyn food importer, to pick up some staples along the way.

My grocery bags and I were crossing Smith Street when we were approached by a diminutive man dressed in wrinkled brown pants and a navy blue T-shirt with Picasso's signature emblazoned across the front. The shirt's a bit of a cliché; you've seen it before. That stated, Lachlan looked good; I looked like God-knows-what, not being one to doll up for Dr. DiLeonibus. I was wearing a yellow corduroy skirt with purple elephant appliqués on it, Jack Rogers sandals, and a white T-shirt; preppy ironic, you could call it, if you were in the mood to be kind. My hair was most likely unclean, and I was trying to hide the whole package behind black sunglasses. Lachlan wore sunglasses with tiny oval lenses trimmed in blue. His hair was short with long sideburns; the gray may have been premature. I quickly assessed his age to be somewhere between thirty-eight and forty-eight. He was walking a dog.

"Can you tell me where I could find *Time Out*?" he asked in an accent that sounded Scottish, referring to the city arts and culture weekly, a spin-off of a magazine that originated in London.

Because I liked the way he looked, and I'm not immune to the accent, I was exceptionally helpful and talkative. I had a lot of information to impart. Finding *Time Out* in that particular corner of Brooklyn was complicated business. Lachlan was fortunate that he chose me to ask. In hindsight, it was probably the single best move he ever made.

"You have two options," I told him. "Both are equidistant from here. There's Barnes and Noble over there"—I pointed in a northwesterly direction—"or Book Court, over there"—I pointed in a southwesterly direction. Then I concluded: "Book Court is probably your best bet with the dog, because they keep the magazines right up front by the door; you could grab one and pay for it with one hand and hold the leash and the dog outside with the other. Where are you from?"

"Scotland."

"Really? All my favorite bands are from Scotland."

I blurted that out to keep the conversation going, but it also happened to be true.

"I like American bands," he said. "Last week I went to see Kansas."

That was a bold admission. For me to say I liked Kansas wasn't too much of a stretch. My brother Nick was obsessed with them when he was a teenager, and I guess you could say they rubbed off on me. I know all the lyrics to "Point of Know Return" and "Carry On Wayward Son," as well as to some of their lesser-known songs and B-sides. A man who would go see Kansas at B. B. King's House of Blues by himself was one I wanted to know. The action spoke of a sincere lack of interest in being cool, and yet Lachlan seemed pretty cool. At least he did to me. How often do two people with an appreciation for the prog rock artistry of Kansas find each other on a street corner?

"Thursday, I'm going to see Steely Dan at Jones Beach."

Now I didn't want just to know him, I wanted to go to that concert with him. I had to keep talking.

"What do you do?" I asked.

"I'm a writer," he told me. "I had a novel published ten years ago that sold eighty-two copies in America. I'm here working on my second and third novels."

"I work in publishing," I said. "We should get your book published here."

That was the clincher, as I knew it would be.

"Do you want to meet for coffee later or dinner sometime this week?" he asked.

"Sure."

"Can we meet this week?"

It was the third week in August, and every one of my friends was away. I could not have been more available socially or romantically.

"My schedule is flexible," I said coyly, and handed him my card.

Lachlan read my name. "You're Italian? *Parli italiano?*" he said, then he launched into such fluent Italian that I had a hard time keeping up. When he spoke, he took on the look and manner of an Italian. There was some real serendipity at work as each moment of our encounter revealed a new commonality. Not only was Lachlan an adorable Brit; he could transform himself into a rather appealing Italian. Meeting him on a street corner, while walking home from the dentist in the last lonely days of summer, was nothing short of a miracle.

In our brief conversation, I learned that Lachlan was from Edinburgh but had spent many years in Italy, where he taught English to Italians. He was in the States for the summer, subletting an apartment in Williamsburg with Steve, an American friend he knew from London. Lachlan was dog-sitting for Steve's sister in her big house in Boerum Hill.

The dog's name was Goose, but I mistook it for Gus for the next four months, although that would hardly prove to be my biggest mistake in those months.

I checked my e-mail the second I got home. No word from Lachlan yet, but I knew I would hear from him soon. I made lunch with the supplies I had picked up and some of the ripe summer tomatoes and basil I'd bought at the farmer's market that takes place every Saturday just steps from my apartment. By August, those stalls are bursting with beautiful red, yellow, and orange peppers, big shiny purple eggplants, fragrant bunches of basil, gorgeous ripe tomatoes—it is a cook's playground, and I had no one to cook for.

By the time I was done eating, an e-mail had arrived from Lachlan. He sent his phone number and asked me to call. When we spoke, he wanted to meet right away. He was going to a reading at four; it was now two, could we meet at three? I didn't want to rush, so I suggested we meet for a drink after the reading.

Lachlan agreed to that while expressing concern about missing the evening meal. "It will be dinnertime," he said. "I have some Barilla pasta; you could come here and I could cook for us."

I liked the way his mind worked, but I wasn't so sure about going to a stranger's house to eat a lesser brand of pasta. For De Cecco, I might have considered it, but Barilla, which costs ninety-nine cents a pound at my supermarket, reeked of seediness.

Lachlan's attitude was familiar when he called that evening. The reading was disappointing, the audience questions uninspired. After ten minutes or so spent discussing our options, we made a plan to meet at the corner where we'd met earlier that day; from there we'd find a place to grab a beer. I took the bus from Park Slope for our rendezvous and wondered along the way why there'd been no Scotsmen waiting for me on Boerum

Hill street corners during the decade and a half I lived there.

Lachlan arrived just as I did; he seemed delighted when he saw me, smiling as if happily astonished at how pretty I was. At least, that was what I decided. He kept turning to look at my face as we walked side by side. I had cleaned up considerably since earlier in the day and was looking my date best in an Esprit sundress with an African print I had bought many years before for a date with a guy who dumped me the very night I debuted the dress. Nevertheless, it is one that garners a good deal of compliments, which leads me to conclude that that guy was a fool; the dress is short with a low back and a high front. It says sexy, but only in a whisper.

I slid in right next to Lachlan on the banquette, rather than across from him, when we sat down at Robin des Bois, a French bistro with thrift shop decor. I have no idea why I did this. I suppose the fact that he was in town for only a couple of weeks gave me the sense of having nothing to lose. We were talking books—Lachlan was reading *The Tipping Point;* I viewed this choice as banal but was willing to let it slide, he being a foreigner. I proudly announced that I was reading *The Elementary Particles.* I thought this novel, by Michel Houellebecq, the bad boy of contemporary French literature, would lend me a worldly and sexually daring air, but Lachlan dismissed Houellebecq out of hand, saying: "His novels depict a cold world."

Over pints of Stella Artois, Lachlan told me he had studied philosophy at the University of Aberdeen, then dropped out of a PhD program at the London School of Economics. A small Scottish entity issued his first and theretofore only published novel shortly after that. For most of the past twenty-some-odd years, he lived in Italy, though I also gathered from our conversation that he had spent a year or two in Prague and an unspecified amount of time in Paris. The year before he came to the States, he was living in Edinburgh. He had never lived in Spain but was thinking about it.

Lachlan broke into Italian for part of our conversation; it just so happens that my Italian improves as I drink. By the second beer I was quasifluent, and Lachlan was holding my hand. By the third I didn't have to speak anymore, we were kissing.

Our hands remained joined on the short walk to the place where he was staying. We were going there to smoke: me a cigarette, Lachlan pot. Goose inhabited a very nice brownstone. We walked into a giant parlor encompassing the living room and kitchen. On the counter dividing the two spaces was a basket full of fruit and vegetables, but there was no time to partake of the produce. Lachlan led me right downstairs to the bedroom, where he kept his smoking apparatus—a practical, no-frills pipe made from a plastic takeout container covered with foil that had tiny pinholes punched into one side. He placed a pinch of dope over the holes, lit it, and inhaled from a larger hole on the other side. Not exactly suave, but Lachlan was more cute and elflike than dashing. There was nothing he could do that would turn me off. When he made a move to exhale smoke from his mouth to mine, it was so alluring that I couldn't resist.

Lachlan lit votive candles that lined the dresser and nightstand. He put a home-made CD in the small boom box on the dresser. Electronica came pouring out— booming beats and the occasional chant. Lachlan announced his erotic game plan with a flourish, and though the sound track is not what I would have chosen, every other decision he made was spot on. The music and sex played in a con-tinual loop until we broke for a snack.

Lachlan was a cook. But at this point he revealed his originality only in bed and with American breakfast cereals. He poured himself a bowl of raisin bran, added a few extra tablespoons of raisins, a bunch of almonds, some walnuts, and a shot or two of honey, then poured milk over the concoction. I took my cereal plain with milk. We ate standing at the kitchen counter.

"Did I pick you up or did you pick me up?" I asked.

"I think it was mutual," Lachlan replied.

We talked for a while longer, then I wanted to go home. I'm comfortable doing lots of things with strangers—sleeping isn't one of them. But Lachlan insisted I stay, so I stayed. When we woke up, somehow on the other side of the bed, I was less unnerved than I thought I'd be. In fact, I was surprised at how at ease I was, until Lachlan asked me if I had ever been married.

I'm always taken aback when I get that question. My first reaction is that I'm too young to have been married, though in actuality I'm old enough to have been married and have seven children and maybe even a divorce or two under my belt. I am aware that my amazement is merely a film covering countless difficult feelings of failure and confusion over the matter.

I gave my stock answer, one that I hope masks my stirring emotions and probably fails:

"No, I haven't gotten around to that yet."

"Who was your last boyfriend?"

"Can't this just happen in a vacuum?" I asked.

"Nothing ever does," Lachlan replied.

I asked Lachlan how old he was (forty-six). I told him how old I was (forty). Lachlan's last girlfriend was an Australian painter (I'm imagining twenty-eight). That seemed so cool and exotic (and young). I felt bland (and old).

"I would like to see you again," he said. I agreed, suggesting I accompany him to Steely Dan. Lachlan had only one ticket and didn't want to buy another. If I got just one for me, we wouldn't be sitting together, so I bought two more and figured we'd find someone we could sell Lachlan's to before the show. Not that the money made any difference; this summer, which began with me dating a dreary fellow not worth mentioning, was becoming lovely beyond my wildest imaginings—that was worth any number of Steely Dan tickets.

We got out of bed, and Lachlan made coffee. He toasted Pepperidge Farm whole-wheat bread and buttered it with salty butter for me. It could not have been more delicious if it had been an omelet oozing with Beluga caviar and crème fraîche. We hung out for a while, chatting and drinking coffee—since my boss was away for the month, I was in even less of a rush than usual to get to the office. When eleven rolled around, I started to consider showing my face.

At noon, when I arrived at the NoHo offices of *Harper's Magazine,* evidence of Ginia's phone calls were all over the place—on my cell phone, on my office voice mail, on my home voice mail. I took my time getting back to her, taking a few moments to savor the night before for myself.

"On my way home from the dentist I met the most adorable Scotsman you have ever seen. We're going to have coffee!" I had written her the minute I walked in the door after it occurred. It was only right for her to be curious about our date. In fact, as my best friend, she was obligated to care. I would have been disappointed if she didn't. So I called and told her as much as I could, hinting at the sex, crowing about Steely Dan.

I assumed I'd see Lachlan before the concert, still two days away. When I was done with my exercise class that evening, there was a message from him on my cell phone.

"Did you make the bed?" I asked when I returned the call. The sheets were in disarray when I left in the morning. Considering it unseemly to leave a borrowed house in such chaos, I offered to fix it—this was my neurosis, after all—but Lachlan insisted that he would take care of it.

"No," he answered, "I want to mess them up again."

In under an hour, I was back on the bus.

It's always a little shocking to see someone you've been on a date with (and then some) for the second time. They are never quite how you remembered them. Lachlan seemed unnerved, moving quickly and jerkily when he greeted me at the door. As this is usually my role in relationships, I found myself in the unfamiliar position of being the serene one. He took my hand and led me straight to the bedroom, even though it was only nine-thirty. There he had re-created the previous night's scene. The candles were lit, and Groove Armada was blaring from the little boom box on the dresser: "If you're fond of sand dunes and salty air . . . ," went "At the River," the one familiar tune I heard in those evenings.

Almost in line with the number of times

I have prepared elaborate meals for men is
the number of times I have been implored
to read book reviews drawn from conveniently stashed (in the drawer near the bed,
in the messenger bag that just happened to
come along to the restaurant) folders and
envelopes. Yes, Lachlan had brought his
over from Edinburgh, and out they came
the next morning. I was to read them in
bed before coffee. I find it tough enough
to focus on book reviews under ideal circumstances, while lying on my own couch
in the sanctuary of my own apartment on
a Sunday afternoon. Post-early-relationship
sex, it is nearly impossible. I attempted to
follow a couple of lines, forced a chortle or
two, then scrambled to come up with some
clever comment, like, "Ha, funny that he's
buried in a peat bog," as if I had a clue as to
what a peat bog was.

"Can you? Can you really help me with
my book?" Lachlan asked.

I racked my brain thinking up literary
agents who might take my call. There
was an old friend of Ethan's who played

drums in our band; I could try him. And a chubby guy who never called me again after I took him to see the Magnetic Fields; that *had* to count for a favor. "There are some people I could ask," I told him.

I had no idea if I could help, but I supposed I would have to try because I was already madly in love with Lachlan.

He took my hands. "I don't want any of this to get in the way of our friendship."

"I appreciate you saying that," I said, well aware that it was, in fact, in the way.

While Lachlan was making my breakfast and giving me the rundown on the novel he was working on, a voice in my head that sounded a lot like mine said, *This man will never love you.* I told the voice to shut up and went full speed ahead with him to Jones Beach Theater for Steely Dan.

Lachlan had planned to take the train out there, but I put an end to that. We'd borrow my mother's car and leave in the afternoon in order to have an hour or two on the beach before the show. I'd take the day off from work to pick up the car in the morning and squeeze an exercise class in there somewhere, too. I forgot to bring my cell phone with me and returned home to find six messages from Lachlan in a variety of formats: text, voice mail, he'd even tried to page me.

"Have you eaten?" he asked when I got back to him. "I have lunch for you if you haven't." No man has ever "had lunch for me." He sounded like my mother, and that wasn't bad, but I wanted to get on the road. I turned down his offer, and Lachlan upped the ante with a significantly less maternal request:

"Come over and take a shower with me."

Lachlan got his way—however, with my car parked at a meter fed with only enough change to buy us thirty minutes, we had to move fast. We succeeded in making both love and pasta within the time limit. Lachlan prepared a sauce of tomatoes and eggplant for a picnic on the beach. We got out of bed and scrambled to prepare rigatoni and make it out of the house before the meter ran out, but Lachlan was visibly collapsing under the pressure. He dropped a plate that shattered all over the kitchen floor, and while he was sweeping up the shards of glass, he remembered that he hadn't fed the dog and the pasta still had to be packed up. "Can you do this? Can you do this for me?" he said, handing me a plastic container and a ladle. Lachlan did not yet know that I could outmother him any day of the week.

We made it to the car with a minute to spare, so we spent it at the deli buying M&M's, Twizzlers, and Coca-Cola for the trip. My kilt had a sweet tooth. He wanted Häagen-Dazs ice cream, too, but they didn't have sticky toffee pudding, his preferred flavor, so we didn't get any.

At last we were off, racing past the grand Brooklyn Museum and gloriously faded apartment buildings of Eastern Parkway, blasting AC/DC's album *Back in Black,* with Lachlan shouting some lyrics from the car window: "Honey, whattaya do for money?"

I know what music to play for my boy-friends, and I know what to feed them; the third thing I pride myself on is an unfailing sense of direction. I rarely get lost. I can feel my way to just about any-where, and when I miss the road, I find my way back to the right one quickly. Not so on this trip. I ended up on the Northern Parkway when I should have been on the Southern, and the little connecting roads I count on to take me from one to the other were nowhere to be found. I don't adhere to my gender in that oft-cited difference between men and women—I *hate* asking for directions and refuse to do it. But as I noticed the sun making its way west ahead of us, I broke down and called Ginia, who grew up near Jones Beach and could put us on the right path. To get on it, I made some hairpin turns that scared the bejesus out of Lachlan. I tried to reassure him that he was safe with me. "I'm a great driver, really! I can't believe I'm lost, I don't know why this is happening." Lachlan, feisty from sugar, ribbed me relentlessly in Italian.

Translated from the original Italian:

"When I saw you at that street corner, you looked like a nice, responsible woman. You were carrying bags of groceries, so I assumed you were married, possibly with a couple of kids. You gave me a card that read 'Vice President,' so I thought you were a sensible career women. But what are you!? You sleep until eleven, go to work at noon, you don't know how to drive, and you don't know where you're going!"

He was right about that last part. I hadn't a clue where I was going.

What I did know was that minutes later I was sitting beside the ocean with delectable Lachlan. I had brought along a bottle of Chianti I had been saving for a special occasion—carefully packed in ice so that it would maintain cellar temperature—but I had to drink it by myself. Turned out Lachlan had some health issues that restricted his alcohol intake—a problem with his "bile tube" a few years back, which led to a lengthy hospitalization in Rome, a consultation with one of the pope's physicians, and the discovery of an arrhythmia that he now took a daily pill to regulate. While I sipped, Lachlan sparked up his pot, an indulgence that apparently didn't affect his "bile tube" function.

As you can imagine, I'm a bit of a snob when it comes to pasta, so I didn't have much faith in what Lachlan could churn out in his borrowed kitchen. My prejudice was misguided; his rigatoni with eggplant was scrumptious, so much so that I have since duplicated the dish many times, and I can't say I do it any better than he did.

~~~ ~~~ ~~~ ~~~

Lachlan's Rigatoni with Eggplant

Delicious hot or cold.

3 tablespoons olive oil, plus a bit extra if needed

1/2 medium yellow onion, chopped
Pinch hot red pepper flakes
I large eggplant, cut into 1/2-inch cubes
2 teaspoons salt
1 large (28-ounce) can crushed tomatoes
1/4 cup red wine
1 tablespoon sugar (eggplant is acidic!)
1 pound rigatoni
1 cup basil leaves, torn
Freshly grated parmigiano

Heat olive oil in a large skillet over medium heat; add onion and red pepper and sauté until the onion is almost translucent. Add the eggplant and 1 teaspoon salt and cook for 20 minutes, allowing the vegetables to get a little brown. Then add the tomatoes, wine, sugar, and remaining salt and cook for 50 to 60 minutes, until the eggplant is very soft.

Cook the rigatoni according to the directions for pasta on page 32. When the pasta is drained, add it to the skillet with the eggplant if it fits; otherwise return it to the pasta pot and add a few ladlefuls of sauce, a dash of olive oil, and the torn basil leaves.

Ladle into bowls garnished with a dollop of extra sauce and a few basil leaves. Serve with grated parmigiano.

Serves 4 as a main course, 6 as a first.

Lachlan wanted to *know* me. As we reclined on the beach, he grilled me on my childhood and past relationships, things I wasn't ready to talk about with a man I liked so much but knew so briefly. "Could you at least fill me in up to age sixteen?" he pleaded. Since his attentions were half-consumed with the smoke of a ship he thought he saw far off near the horizon line, I told him about the trip my family took to Italy on a ship called the *Raffaello* well before my twelfth birthday. Lachlan's parents had sailed to the United States on the *Queen Elizabeth II* and were coming back next year on the *Queen Mary*. He talked about their travels abroad and a less exotic trip the family recently made to Liverpool for his brother's wedding. That event relieved Lachlan of some of the parental pressure on him to settle down, especially now that his sibling had produced an heir. The ship Lachlan was tracing turned out to be nothing more than a shadow. The focus on this trivial disappointment was enough to push us on our way to the show.

We traversed a Scotland-size parking lot to get to the theater. Lachlan, now stoned, was amazed by its enormity and that of the bottom of a middle-aged man in pink Dockers whom he called a blanc-mange. We felt positively youthful as we followed him along with a throng of potbellied fifty-somethings making their way to the show. His comments had me in tears, even the ones directed at me for thinking we could sell our extra ticket to one of these people.

"Giulia, I don't think '*Dan fans*' show up at a concert looking to buy a ticket.

'Dan fans' are a little more organized than that!" he teased.

Jones Beach Theater is both giant food court and arena. Lachlan's munchies were calling once again for Häagen-Dazs ice cream, but there was only Carvel. I got a sundae of vanilla with hot fudge, which Lachlan, while remarking on its poor quality, ate most of. Meanwhile, Michael McDonald of Doobie Brothers fame was doing his opening act, banging on keyboards and singing "What a Fool Believes." We could see him on the giant screen as we waited in line for coffee at the Starbucks stand. Lachlan decided that McDonald looked like Kenny Rogers, so for the rest of the night we referred to him as Ken, yelping out his new name when he came back out on the stage with "the Dan" to sing backup vocals on "Peg."

Lachlan was amazed that I was able to find the car, now all alone in an empty graph of white lines by the time we got to it. We didn't get lost on the way home, either; all the signs pointed to New York, and we followed them. "I'm still amazed when I see signs for New York, I can't believe I'm here," Lachlan said, squeezing my hand. I couldn't believe it, either.

The next week, Lachlan came to stay with me for the remainder of his trip and I took the rest of the summer off from work. I called my mother to tell her she wouldn't be seeing me for a while; I had fallen in love with a Scotsman, a Scotsman who loved Italy and spoke fluent Italian, and could I keep the car? Up till then, the only vacation I had in mind was a few days off, during which I wouldn't go much farther than Prospect Park. I couldn't afford to travel, having just spent a bundle on my apartment and things to fill it with. Lachlan fell into my lap, a *scoti ex machina* who made my world as exotic as Dundee (to me; I've never seen it) and cozy as a rented cottage on the Outer Hebrides by way of Capri.

He and his rucksack showed up at my apartment on a sticky, hot Monday afternoon after an arduous journey from Williamsburg, where my soul mate made a lunch of spaghetti Bolognese for his roommate, Steve, then said good-bye to him and their sublet. I worked that day, my last until after Labor Day, and rushed home to meet Lachlan, who got off at the wrong subway stop, ended up on the opposite end of Prospect Park, and arrived at my door sweaty and exhausted from the long trek. I tried to soothe him with music, playing an album by a new heavy rock band called Wolfmother that Kit had recommended. Lachlan dubbed the effort "inauthentic" and asked instead if I had his favorite Led Zeppelin album, *Physical Graffiti*. I owned every Led Zeppelin album *except Physical Graffiti*, but *Led Zeppelin II* or *Houses of the Holy* would not suffice. He wanted to hear *Physical Graffiti*, and I wanted to provide it for him. I assumed a click or two on iTunes would have "Custard Pie" coming out of my speakers in no time, but such simplicity was not to be: iTunes did not carry the Zeppelin catalog (a problem that has since been rectified). I pondered how I could fulfill his musical request and provide a palatable dinner. The undertaking left no time for a trip to the store, so I settled on bucatini amatriciana, a dish whose ingredients (onions, pancetta, canned tomatoes, bucatini) I always have on hand. Fortunately, Lachlan was not a man opposed to eating two pastas in one day.

The *Physical Graffiti* problem was a more stubborn one. I clicked on LimeWire, a free file-sharing program Kit had put onto my computer that I had never used. I believe in paying for my music, but this bad business decision on the part of Plant and Page left me no choice. LimeWire wouldn't open, having died from neglect. I put up a pot of water to boil for pasta, then began to follow the steps to resuscitate it. This took longer than I remembered it taking for Kit, and soon enough the water was boiling. Amatriciana is a simple sauce that can be made while the pasta is cooking, but it gets a heck of a lot more complicated if you try to make it while downloading mp3 file-sharing technology onto your laptop.

〜〜〜〜〜〜〜〜

Bucatini Amatriciana with MP3 File-Sharing Technology

   1 iBook G4
   1 tablespoon olive oil
   2 slices pancetta
   1 small onion
   1 Visa card
   1 (16-ounce) can choppped tomatoes
   Salt
   1/2 pound bucatini
   1/4 cup freshly grated pecorino

Fill a large pot with water and place over high heat.

Attempt to open LimeWire from the icon on your desktop. Fail.

The Scotsman in the apartment, who is useless with computers but, as we know, is capable of helping with pasta, will retreat to the bathroom for a shower.

Go to the LimeWire Web site and follow the steps to download the software onto iBook G4. This will take much longer than you think. Water is now boiling, and you haven't done a thing for the sauce. Leave installation running, go to kitchen, and start sauce.

Heat olive oil in skillet over medium heat; chop pancetta, add it to oil, and let it get a little crispy. Meanwhile, chop the onion and then add it to the pancetta.

Return to desk to check on the installation. Discover that installation of free software is not happening; you will have to upgrade to LimeWire Pro. Retrieve Visa card and type account number in appropriate box; learn what "security code" is.

Run back to kitchen, where pancetta and onions should be a little more browned than you needed them to be. Tell yourself that caramelization is a good thing; add half the tomatoes and their juices, let them thicken a bit, and return to desk.

Adding the credit card numbers worked! You are ready to download songs.

Scotsman is finished with shower, drying himself, and calling out his requests. He will have his heart set on "Custard Pie." Search for "Custard Pie" and click to download song, then run back to the kitchen.

Add the rest of the tomatoes to the skillet. Add salt to the boiling water, then the bucatini; give the pot a stir and go back to the computer.

You will find a notice telling you the song cannot be downloaded, as it "needs more sources." Deliver news to Scotsman, now emerging from bathroom. See how he feels about "In My Time of Dying," find that it won't do, attempt "Custard Pie" again, fail. Go on to other songs from *Physical Grafitti*—find "The Rover," "Kashmir," "Ten Years Gone," "Bron-Yr-Aur," and download all without a hitch.

By now, you have forgotten the boiling pasta. Run to the kitchen to taste it; it will be overcooked. You will be ashamed for having failed at everything. Drain immediately, add to sauce. Remove from heat, sprinkle with pecorino.

Serves 2, unsatisfyingly.

I was shaken by the fact that the first thing I ever cooked for Lachlan was a sorry example of my abilities. Overcooked pasta is the cardinal sin of Italian cookery—*sfatta*, my mother calls it in what may be her own Sicilian dialect—my knowledge of Italian translates the word to something like "mismade." I pouted over the meal, knowing I could do so much better. Lachlan faulted himself for getting in the shower right at the crucial moment. This would be the only time he took responsibility for a limp noodle.

"Do you want me to make coffee?" I asked Lachlan when we awoke the next morning.

"Only if you want me to be eternally grateful," was his reply.

Imagine that sentence, spoken in a mild Scottish accent, and maybe you can understand why I loved him as much as I did.

The meals got better. Once free from that time-suck known as the office, I could devote my days to planning them. I shopped in the morning while Lachlan "inserted a few cherries" into his novel before giving it to me to read. I was in heaven, exploring my new neighborhood in the quiet daytime hours, checking out the food markets, determining where the good cheese was to be found, who had the best meat and who the better bread. I returned with all manner of delicious things for us to eat when Lachlan was ready to break for lunch. I knew he would enjoy my discoveries just as much as I.

I returned to find him writing and laughing away to himself.

"Helloooo," he shouted when I walked in the door.

I went to the kitchen to assemble an array of lovely things for us to have for lunch. I couldn't stop smiling as I made him a tuna salad that was a lunchtime staple back in the Shelter Island days.

～～ ～～ ～～ ～～

Summerhouse Tuna Salad

(Adapted from Ginia Bellafante)

1 6-ounce can tuna, packed in olive oil

1 tablespoon chopped red onion

1 summer tomato, seeded and chopped

1 teaspoon capers

1 1/2 teaspoons olive oil

1/4 teaspoon salt

Few grindings pepper

1 tablespoon chopped parsley (and/or basil if you have it)

Open tuna and drain the excess oil, put it in a bowl, and add the chopped onion, tomato, capers, olive oil, salt, and pepper. Mix it all up and garnish with the chopped parsley.

Serve with fresh bread.

Serves 2; easily doubled.

I served it with bread that was still warm when I bought it, slices of soppressata—laid out in neat strips on a whimsical plate decorated with a childish drawing of a squirrel—olives, and fresh mozzarella. I presented our feast on a tray I had bought the previous day at the Brooklyn Museum—all the better to serve him with.

My apartment was so sunny, we may as well have been outside. Lachlan drank water, and I had a glass of red wine, slightly chilled for our indoor picnic.

"Buon appetito," Lachlan said before digging in.

"Buon appetito," I said back to him, beaming.

We said that to each other before every meal, even when we were no longer beaming.

While we ate, Lachlan continued with the big questions:

"Do you have any regrets?"

"Do you have everything you want?"

"Where do you see yourself in ten years?"

"Do you ever want to get married?"

"Do you think about having children?"

I didn't know what to tell him. Did I have everything I wanted? Everything except a husband. Where did I see myself ten years from now? I saw myself married—same place I saw myself ten years ago—clearly my vision is blurry. Did I think about having children? Not often, but I would entertain the idea for Lachlan. How much to divulge became a philosophical question for me. What knowledge of my past relationships was Lachlan entitled to? I couldn't think of anything to say that wouldn't implicate me as unlovable.

I wasn't eager to bring past disappointments into a new relationship that seemed full of possibility. We were getting on well together, we agreed on everything from music to pasta shapes to ice-cream flavors. Everything, that is, except for air-conditioning—Lachlan reviled it, dubbing the machine "the noisy fridge." He composed a little protest song set to the tune of Kansas's "Point of Know Return." In the middle of the night, he woke me up singing: "Your motherrrrr, she says it's freeeeezing." I nearly wet the bed I was laughing so hard, but I didn't give in. There is only so far that I will bend to the European sensibility.

Although I embrace the comforts of the New World, I'm old-fashioned when it comes to cooking. I wouldn't let Lachlan do any, even though he was more than capable. Instead I relegated him to menial tasks, like chopping an onion or garlic, which he happened to do beautifully; I can't claim knife skills so refined. He didn't put up a fight, he was mellowed by the pot he'd smoke while keeping me company in the kitchen—always closing the shutters so the neighbors wouldn't see. We'd listen to music; I'd even let him play his. That electronica stuff was growing on me, especially Zero 7, whose song "Destiny" I considered our song, though I wouldn't admit anything so precious to Lachlan.

Not that he refrained from habitually marveling over what a thing it was that we met. "You can't call it fate, but chance," he would say, taking me in his arms. I'd point out two tiny prep bowls I'd picked up for ten cents each at Fishs Eddy on my way home from the dentist, items I considered to be major players in that event. "If I hadn't stopped to buy these bowls, it would never have happened," I'd say, floored by the idea that my future had been determined by two ten-cent prep bowls. Ah, those little bowls. I get a bit sad when I look at them now, but I haven't gotten rid of them; they are essential to my *mise en place*.

Earlier that summer, during the five minutes I wallowed in disappointment over the utter uselessness of my latest fling, I went to visit my friend Jennifer

Romanello on Long Island. Jennifer shares a beach cabana with her extended family, all fabulous cooks staunchly dedicated to eating and drinking well. From a tiny hot plate, they create incredibly sophisticated dishes, risotto and porcini, linguine with crabmeat. One I took particular note of was a stew of colorful sautéed peppers made by Jennifer's sister Carmela. I marveled at her skillful hand on the paring knife as she cut up peppers along with red onion and tomato and let them slip into the pot. I re-created this dish for Lachlan with gorgeous peppers from the farmer's market.

～～ ～～ ～～ ～～

Carmela Romanello's Sautéed Summer Peppers

2 tablespoons olive oil

1 clove garlic, minced

1 red onion, ends removed, sliced lengthwise into semicircular chunks

Pinch dried oregano

3 bell peppers (1 red, 1 orange, 1 yellow), cored,
    seeds and pith removed, cut into strips
1 1/4 teaspoons salt
1 large tomato (or 2 plum tomatoes), seeded
    and cut into chunks
1/4 cup torn basil leaves
Freshly ground pepper

Heat olive oil in large sauté pan or Dutch oven over medium heat and sauté garlic and onion with the oregano until the onion is soft and translucent, about 3 to 5 minutes. Add peppers and 1 teaspoon salt and cook partially covered, stirring occasionally, for 15 to 20 minutes. Add tomatoes and 1/4 teaspoon salt; continue to cook another 10 to 15 minutes until the peppers are very soft. Test for seasoning and serve with torn basil leaves and freshly ground pepper.

Serve with Italian sausages, barbecued if you're lucky enough to have outdoor space. I am not, so I grill them on the stove.

Yield: 6 servings.

I took Lachlan to Bay Ridge, where I showed him the house I grew up in and my favorite butcher shop, Faicco. I bought us heaps of food—steaks, sausages, bacon, cheese. I love the sight of the gorgeous meat laid out neatly behind the refrigerated glass. I like giving the guy behind the counter my big order, like a signora from days gone by. The dishes I made for Lachlan were simple, but the way he reacted to them, you would have thought I was Luciano Pavarotti's personal chef. A particular revelation for Lachlan was orzo, a pasta shaped like rice he had never before tried. It makes a great summer side dish, as it's delicious warm or cool. I made this one with steaks grilled on the stove and seasoned with a little olive oil and salt and pepper.

~~~~~~~~

Orzo with Cherry Tomatoes and Basil

1/2 cup orzo

1 tablespoon olive oil

1 cup cherry tomatoes (a mix of red and yellow if the latter are available), halved

1/4 cup thinly sliced fresh basil

2 tablespoons pine nuts, toasted

1 teaspoon red wine vinegar

Salt and pepper to taste

Cook the orzo according to the directions for pasta on page 32. Note: Orzo cooks quicker than regular pastas, so check it earlier than you normally would; 6 minutes seems reasonable to me. Drain the pasta and add the oil. Once it is cooled, stir in the tomatoes, basil, pine nuts, vinegar, and salt and pepper to taste.

Yield: 2 servings.

Lachlan continued with his questions over the sausage and peppers and the steak and orzo. He asked them on walks through the rain to the museum and on sunny days lying in Prospect Park. I continued my campaign to evade.

"Why is it necessary for me to share all that?" I asked.

"Well, if we were to get married, I would want to know."

Those were the magic words. I revealed highlights from just about every chapter in this book.

When I inquired about his brushes with marriage, I got vague answers:

"You can imagine that at my age, I've come close to getting married."

For Lachlan, the one who got away was Claire. He lived with her in London in the late 1980s, and their alleged roller coaster banged on its tracks until the mid-1990s. As Lachlan tells it, Claire was depressed. When she took her meds she was wonderful; when she didn't she alternated between flinging herself at him and sending him away. They broke up and got back together many times in those years in which they shared a single bed in a London studio that Lachlan would sporadically leave for Italian mattresses. They could never see each other without "ending up in bed together," he told me.

The line gave me pause—our sex life had slowed down considerably since he'd moved in. I told him it hurt me to hear about Claire, in light of the near halt. "How old was I then?" Lachlan replied by way of explanation. True, that was many years ago, but he was hardly in the Viagra demographic, and we had only gotten started.

It was distressing to learn that what Lachlan really liked to do in bed was sleep. He was a champion napper, constantly tired. After a good ten-to-twelve-hour night of rest, he'd be ready for a lie-down shortly after breakfast. I'm awfully fond of sleep myself and have found it nearly impossible to get out of bed every morning of my entire life, but once

I'm up, I'm up for the day. I hardly ever nap, and whenever I do, I find it so trying to wake up again that it's just not worth it. While Lachlan took his *pennichella* (as he called it), I reclined on the living room sofa, reading his novel, now ready for my eyes. His cleverly titled book was about a rhinoceros that turns into a human being and slips unnoticed into a group of Englishmen on safari in South Africa. (Okay, every detail of that description has been changed so as not to reveal Lachlan's identity, but what I've written conveys the spirit of the work. It was experimental literature.) When he awoke, he wanted to know exactly where I was in the manuscript. I would point out the page, and he would grab it out of my hands and start reading it aloud, laughing hysterically. I laughed neither as hard nor as often as he did.

The novel was witty and inventive, a riot of language completely devoid of any genuine situation or emotion. I found it to be as accomplished as many I had worked on in my career, if not better than most of them. It deserved to be published, but I could see where it needed a tweak or two. It wasn't quite ready, but it had the potential to be a book I might show to an agent without shame. Lachlan would have to work on it while he was in Italy, which is where he was headed next. His first stop was the home of his friend Ruth in the mountains near the Swiss border. Ruth, who was Irish, used to teach English with Lachlan in Rome, then she married an Italian widower who whisked her away to the Alps. Lachlan reckoned he could stay with them for a few weeks; he didn't know where he was going from there. His intention was to sort out his books and other possessions that were scattered throughout Italy in basements and attics of other British females who once taught English and married Italians. (Why hadn't I thought of that?) Along the way, he would see if there was an Italian city where he might consider building a bookshelf of his own.

"Maybe I should come and live in New York," he would say every other day. That was my wish, but I dared not say it. I dreaded his departure, and he appeared reluctant about it, too. He took lots of pictures of my apartment building. "I feel like this is my home," he'd say.

We brainstormed about what kind of work he could do here. I offered to introduce him to magazine editors; he suggested we open a restaurant together. But the conversation was always dampened by the reality of immigration and visa issues. Two of my colleagues at *Harper's* were foreigners working in the States under a provision known as "extraordinary alien status."

"You could apply for 'extraordinarily sleepy alien' status," I proffered as we considered the options. I always liked the extraterrestrial ring of the term and was delighted to be able to adapt it to Lachlan's particular proclivity. In my attempt to promote the United States as a home for Lachlan, I made this all-American dish: crab cakes that

I served on a bed of mashed potatoes and corn.

~~~~~~~~~~~

Maryland Colony Crab Cakes

(Adapted from *Bon Appétit* magazine)

- 2 tablespoons celery, minced
- 2 tablespoons scallions, green parts only, minced
- 2 tablespoons mayonnaise
- 1 egg
- 1 1/2 teaspoons dijon mustard
- 1/4 teaspoon salt
- 1/8 teaspoon cayenne pepper
- 1/2 pound crabmeat
- 1 1/2 cups panko (or bread crumbs, which are more American, I suppose, but not as good)
- 1 tablespoon olive oil
- 1 tablespoon butter
- 1 lemon, cut into wedges

In a medium bowl, mix together all but the last two ingredients. Shape into 4 small or 2 large patties, according to your mood and spirit of abundance. Refrigerate, covered with plastic wrap, for at least 1 hour.

Over medium heat, fry in olive oil and butter until browned, about 4 minutes per side. Serve with lemon wedges.

Yield: 4 small or 2 large crab cakes.

To continue my public relations campaign, I took him to Philadelphia, birthplace of liberty, a city I know well because my sister Nancy went to college and graduate school there and I used to visit her often. The Philadelphia Museum of Art is one of my favorites, and I wanted to show it to Lachlan. He swooned at the Chardins and topped my connoisseurship of Italian Renaissance art as we toured the galleries hand in hand. When I took him to see Independence Hall and the Liberty Bell, he shook his fists and launched into an amusing tirade about the Founding Fathers being a bunch of tax evaders.

All seemed to be going well with project make-an-American-out-of-Lachlan, then he'd get some notion in his head that would send me into the dumps. "The one thing that holds me back from living here is that there could be a terrorist attack" was one of them.

In addition to Lachlan vacillating about New York as a possible home, we had other customs that developed over the course of those twenty-four days (not that I counted). After Lachlan's nap came coffee and Häagen-Dazs ice cream. We tried every flavor from sticky toffee pudding (good), to banana split (excellent), to caramel cone (out of this world, especially if you were lucky and got lots of cone bits). It rained often, and Lachlan didn't much like leaving the house anyway, so we watched *Da Ali G Show* together. Lachlan had never heard of Sacha Baron Cohen, but once exposed, he couldn't get enough. He affectionately referred to the show as *Dude*. "Should we watch another *Dude*?" he'd say. Borat was his favorite character. It was nearly impossible to get Lachlan out of the apartment between napping and *Dude*. At times I came down with cabin fever and insisted we go for a walk. Lachlan would come along, holding my hand all the way, thanking me for forcing him to go outside. Then he'd crawl into bed immediately upon our return, worn out from the exertion.

Still, for a very tired person, he managed to fit a lot into those days. Lachlan was up for any new situation or person that might stimulate his literary imagination. He carried index cards to take notes for his fiction and brought them along to the bris for Jen and Jeff's baby, Benjamin, who was born a few days after we met. He dragged himself out of bed at seven a.m. for that one and even mustered enough energy to help drag the many gifts from the temple to the car in the pouring rain. "Invite me to the wedding, I give good presents," said Jeff's mother, Estelle. Was it that obvious we were made for each other? We took the subway to Coney Island and the car through the Bronx (which Lachlan found insufficiently threatening). He was up for anything, really, except for sex—with me, at least.

And yet reproduction was very much on his mind.

"We're going to have to be getting on with it if we want to have children, we're both getting old," he said, mulling over the topic of babies on a Sunday stroll.

"Why don't you stay here and we can try to have them together?" I replied, assuming that was what he was getting at.

Lachlan stopped and hugged me. *"Chi sa?"* he said. ("Who knows?")

(I was encouraged. This was more than I ever got from Ethan on the subject.)

"But I need to make money," Lachan said.

"We're working on that. . . . Little Lorenzo Melucci Martyn," I fantasized aloud.

"Would there be a British school we could send him to?"

"Of course, New York has every kind of school."

I had no idea if there was a British school. What would be the point of such a place, anyway, since Brits speak more or less the same language as most Americans—to teach the little kiddies that the country they inhabited was founded by tax evaders?

As much as Lachlan's musings stymied me, they fed my fantasies in those weeks. I could only presume that he was questioning his own path because his love for me had pushed him to rethink his future. Never mind the fact that at forty-six years of age, Lachlan didn't have a home, had never stayed in one place for any significant length of time, and had never committed to a woman. Everybody has to grow up at some point. I had some growing up to do myself. "I can't go on like this forever, and neither can you," he'd say. Why would I not take such assertions to mean that he was ready for a shared life in my Park Slope one-bedroom? That

Lachlan's desperation to be published came from a yearning for a more serious life. I was convinced that we had met to move into the next phase together. I would help him with his career, and he would help me with that marriage and children stuff I was having so much trouble with. Destiny.

I got blue as Lachlan's departure date neared. I'd cry and he would tell me that there was no reason to feel sad. "It's so amazing that we found each other. We've both found a friend, possibly for life." I was only slightly put off by his use of the word *friend*, choosing to see it as something positive—after all, one's husband should also be one's best friend. But if Lachlan wasn't returning, the meeting was no cause for celebration, at least for me.

"I wouldn't be surprised if I came back," he said as he walked out the door of my apartment for what could have been the last time.

"I wouldn't be surprised, either," I replied.

"Then again, there's no point in me coming back if neither of us is surprised."

We arrived at the airport with time to spare thanks to Lachlan's fear of flying and the driving rain. We sat and had coffee at a little espresso bar in a corner of Newark Airport, where Lachlan sat beside me with his arm around my shoulder, staring into my eyes. This resembled the look of love to me, but Lachlan never used that word. "I love you" slipped out of my mouth as we said our final goodbye at the security line. I didn't mean to say it; the words just came out in a tiny voice he may not even have heard.

That night I curled up with Lachlan's first novel, which I had ordered via amazon.uk from a bookstore in Campbelltown, Argyll, the day after I met him. I didn't tell Lachlan I'd bought it, and he didn't tell me he'd spotted it on my shelf and signed it, "With love from the *plage* at Coney Island." The novel was a stream-of-consciousness affair, pretty incomprehensible, and though many of the sentences were dazzling and others rip-roaringly funny, I could barely understand the words that composed them and had to bring both volumes of the *Shorter Oxford* into bed with me, too—and not all of them were in there! I needed all twenty volumes of *The Oxford English Dictionary*, books I do not own and that would have made the bed too crowded anyway. Apparently, my boyfriend was a convoluted genius.

"I can't say I'm over my jet lag," read his first e-mail transmitted from a dial-up on an Italian mountaintop, "but I am filled with such happy memories."

Ardent messages signed "LOVE" and "XXXX" arrived from Lachlan almost daily in the suspenseful weeks that followed. They informed me that I was on his mind all the time—or at least when he wasn't thinking about his book—he imagined me at the farmer's market on Saturday mornings; riding over the Manhattan Bridge on the B train as the sun set on my way home from work; or, at night, covered in Häagen-Dazs ice cream (?). "Bed times and meal times are not the same without you," he wrote. Whatever sentiment he transmitted, I'd multiply by ten and return to him.

For the most part, I was enjoying this particular cliff-hanger. "If he comes back and we get married, I will remember this as the happiest time of my life," I'd say to Ginia. This was an ideal situation for me—to be alone in my beautiful home, the prospect of forever love making its way down the Italian peninsula and not through my refrigerator.

It was my first dinner party season in my new place. I entertained nearly every week. One of the most memorable evenings that fall was a mozzarella competition I thought up with my friend Jesse, a reporter for *The Wall Street Journal*. Jesse and his wife, Nell, who is a writer, lived next door and we often ran into each other at the farmer's market. We talked about putting on this challenge for months and finally got it together just in

time to pair the cheese with the last tomatoes of summer.

There is nothing that compares with the
tangy flavor of mozzarella made with buf-
falo milk; the finest examples come from
where my relatives live in the southern
Italian region of Campania. That cheese is
imported to the States, but by the time it
gets off the plane, it's already way past its
prime. Mozzarella dies under refrigeration.
It has to be eaten the day it's made; thus,
it is better to make do with inferior cow's-
milk mozzarella made locally by hand than
waste money on the imported kind. In the
New York neighborhoods that were once
Italian-American ghettos, there are plenty
of such cheeses to try. Each of my guests
took a section of town—Bensonhurst, Little Italy, Greenwich Village, and Carroll
Gardens—and scanned the *latticini* that
still thrive with the onslaught of the young,
wealthy food enthusiasts who have moved
to these enclaves. We did a blind tasting,
picked a winner, then went on to eat more
courses. I made Lachlan's rigatoni and egg-

plant (recipe page 357) and roasted loin of pork seasoned with rosemary. We had cannoli from a bakery in Dyker Heights for dessert. Everyone got to take home some cheese, even after we'd disposed of the losers. I had a freezer full of mozzarella for months. (The frozen cheese is fine to use for melting in a lasagna, parmigiana, or baked ziti.)

~~~~~~~~~~

Food Club Pork Roast

- 6 garlic cloves
- 1/4 cup fresh rosemary
- 2 teaspoons salt
- Freshly ground pepper
- 1 (4 1/2- to 5-pound) rib section center-cut pork loin (have the butcher bone the meat and then reassemble the roast with string)
- 1 tablespoon olive oil
- 1/2 cup white wine

Preheat oven to 350 degrees.

Mince the garlic and rosemary by hand (or better yet, in a food processor). Mix them in a small bowl with the salt and freshly ground pepper. Rub the meat with olive oil and then the garlic-rosemary mixture. Let it sit at room temperature for 30 minutes.

Place pork fat side up on a rack in roasting pan, then pour white wine over it. Roast in center of the oven until a thermometer registers 140 degrees, about 90 minutes. Remove from oven and let the meat rest on a cutting board, tented with foil, for about 20 minutes before slicing.

Discard string, separate bones from the loin, and slice meat to desired thickness. You may cut the ribs and serve them, too, or save them to add them to a tomato sauce. (Pork ribs add richness to sauce.)

Yield: 6 servings.

The lactose onslaught proved too much even for a sturdy constitution like mine. I awoke the next day with stabbing pains in my stomach, which were exacerbated by an e-mail from Lachlan, whom I hadn't heard from for two days. He had descended the mountain and was now in Milan. "Maybe I could live here," he wrote. I took to my bed. The next day he was in Rome, and a week after that, he was still in the Eternal City, bristling under the stagnancy of Italian culture, which he found "quite stifling if I'm to be honest." I felt positive when he went negative on Italy. As much as I love the land of my ancestors, I didn't want my Scotsman there; I wanted him in New York with me.

Lachlan was concentrating on the novel while living on borrowed couches and Internet connections. Meanwhile, I was doing research on agents at book parties and in phone conversations with editor friends. I couldn't imagine how Lachlan could get any work done the way he was living, and even he would admit from time to time that the lifestyle was dragging on him.

"What are you thinking about the future?" he wrote on a day in which he felt particularly lost.

"I'm thinking about a future with you," I replied, assuming that he was looking for the home I wanted to give him along with the book deal.

"I can't think of any kind of future, all I can think of is finishing my novel. Once that's done I don't mind if I have to sleep under a bridge," he wrote.

Apparently, that bridge was going to connect to a multiplex.

"When is the Borat movie coming out?" Lachlan asked the next morning.

"The Borat movie is coming out in early November."

"Oh, that sounds like very good timing to me," he'd reply, and I'd think, Oh, he's coming back in early November. In retrospect, I realize he didn't have a clue what he was doing, but he enjoyed keeping my hopes up until he made "a very beautiful, rational, and romantic decision," something he was going to do when he was done with the book.

That took seven weeks plus some additional hours of computer fumbling on Lachlan's end. A few simple instructions from me had it on its way, and I stayed up most of the night reading. The novel was polished: less rambling, more funny. Lachlan had pulled it off!

Finding him an agent wouldn't be tough, yet it seemed absolutely grueling. This endeavor was above and beyond the call of duty for any friend; I wouldn't do such a thing for my mother, and she wasn't sending me mixed signals from across the Atlantic. But I was going to do it for our future, the one I thought about while listening to that Zero 7 song on my iPod on the subway every morning: "Even though we're miles apart, we are each other's deeeeeeestinyyyyyyy."

The first agent I called was a friend of a friend I vaguely knew, a formerly hot agent who was getting back on his feet after a little, shall we say, health problem. He was all over the novel as I explained it to him on the phone. He professed himself to be a Scotophile—he had studied in Edinburgh and venerated Sir Walter Scott. "E-mail it over," he said, "I'll get back to you early next week." I put the finishing touches on the cover letter I worked on for two days and had both Kit and Anne edit, and off it went.

As early next week became late next week, and then early the week after that turned to two weeks later, I began to lose hope and added looking for an agent to real estate under the heading of "Things That Are Like Dating." Really, everything in life is like dating—if you didn't get the call, you didn't get the agent (the apartment, the boyfriend). Lachlan sent his support from overseas and slept with his rented phone by his bed just in case there was any breaking news overnight. When I finally screwed up the courage to make the follow-up call, I got the answer I expected. I was bummed, mostly because I didn't want to go through it all again, and who knew how many times I would have to. The prospect of this Sisyphean task made me want to lie down. Instead, I picked up the phone and called the agent I'd had in mind for Lachlan from the very beginning, the one who I knew for sure would get the book, the one I was afraid to call because she was that formidable.

I had worked on some of her eccentric authors in the energetic early days of my book publicity career, and I had done a damn good job with them. But she was a woman with much on her plate, and I didn't expect her to remember me. Her assistant answered, and I left a rambling message with her recounting my history with her boss, then went to lunch. I despaired over making that call in the heat of my devastation, not to mention hunger. I was sure I had blown it and would never hear back.

Lachlan wasn't as crushed by the first rejection as I was, but then, what did he care, he didn't have to do any of the work. Plus, it was in his best interest to keep my spirits up and me on the case.

I was feeling crushed by the weight of his need, a load I alone seemed to be carrying while he sent "pillows and downies and the comfiest mattresses over the Atlantic." I had to escape for a weekend with Jen and Jeff to their house in the Berkshires, where there were plenty of "pillows and downies," but no cell phone signal or wi-fi, just to get a break from him.

Naturally, it was when I was getting a little bloody sick of it all that he started to seriously consider returning.

"I'm reading F. Scott Fitzgerald while staring at a postcard of Park Slope," he wrote after my retreat. I didn't reply; he tried again. "Now, I'm looking at travel sites." *That* got my attention. The flights were expensive, the only affordable ones connected through Heathrow, and Lachlan wanted to limit his takeoffs and landings to as few as possible. He still wasn't sure. Then, "I'm tipping, tipping," he wrote a few hours later. But which way? I wondered.

It would have to be a connecting flight, a connecting flight arriving at JFK that very Saturday. But before he entered his credit card number, he spent a few hours surfing weather sites, interpreting the direction of the winds. "I don't know about the red arrows over the Atlantic," he wrote, describing the seven-day forecast map. By lunchtime he had purchased his ticket. I was so excited, I called Ginia right away. Ginia was weary of Lachlan, and rightly so, but she didn't stomp on my dreams. Right after I hung up with her, THE AGENT called me back. I nervously described the complicated art of Lachlan's novel for her and she was interested! She asked me to messenger the manuscript right over. I was ricocheting off the wall. I called Lachlan immediately, even more excited about having my call returned by THE AGENT than by his imminent return. I couldn't get the right degree of worshipfulness from him over what I had made happen. He didn't know the difference between this agent or that agent or how capable I was. I didn't either, but I was starting to get an idea.

Lachlan was on to more pressing issues for the moment, like how much space he would have in my "cupboard" (British for closet). He had picked up a peacoat and a couple of moldy sweaters while sorting out his things, and they too needed a home. Since mine came complete with four cupboards, I was willing to clear out a quarter of one for him and an entire drawer; that would be plenty.

I bounded out of bed that Saturday morning after a text from Lachlan, who had just taken a Xanax and was waiting to board the plane in Rome, woke me. There were a thousand things to do to prepare for his arrival. I dragged my little rolling shopping bag to the supermarket, where I loaded up on all his favorite foods. I bought a box of clementines and all the ingredients for apple muffins. I spent a blissful afternoon baking in my kitchen in anticipation of reuniting with Lachlan. After ten weeks of wondering, I couldn't believe he was actually on his way back.

~~~~~~~~~~~~~

Welcome Back to the Big Apple Apple Muffins

Butter, softened, for greasing muffin pan

2 cups whole-wheat flour (because Lachlan worries about his health!)

1/2 cup sugar

2 teaspoons baking powder

1/2 teaspoon cinnamon

1/2 cup (1 stick) butter, melted (because Lachlan is too thin!)

1 egg, beaten

1 cup milk

2 medium apples, peeled, cored, and chopped

Preheat oven to 400 degrees. Grease a 12-cup muffin pan with softened butter.

In one large bowl, mix together all the dry ingredients. In another bowl, mix together all the wet ingredients. Add the wet ingredients to the dry and mix with a spoon by hand until just combined, then fold in the chopped apples.

Spoon batter into muffin cups and bake for 20 minutes; cool in pan for 10 minutes and then let sit on cooling rack. Serve warm if you don't have to pick up someone from the airport.

Yield: 12 muffins (if you fill the cups to the rim, as I do, you'll get only 9 muffins from this recipe).

I spotted his silhouette first, a small man with a big pack on his back. When he emerged at the British Airways terminal at JFK, we hugged and Lachlan took my hand the way he always did as we walked to my mother's car.

"When we get home we'll take our clothes off and have a shower and kiss," he said, which was a lot more than I was expecting to hear from him, let alone do with him. Adding two planes and jet lag to the equation of Lachlan's low libido and inclination toward exhaustion under the best of circumstances had me poised for a joyous but chaste reunion. Our stunted sex life had entered my mind while Lachlan was away, but I really didn't care that much about it. Just looking at him made me smile: his elfin face, his slim body wrapped in a boy's-size navy blue Lacoste shirt that was worn and old. I washed that shirt carefully for him and made sure not to put it in the dryer. Lachlan wanted to preserve it, and it merited preservation.

We took a shower and kissed and did all the things that Lachlan's surprising statement implied. Even more astounding was the stack of presents he'd brought for me—there was a rather nice camel-hair scarf, a book of essays by Aldo Buzzi, a little sequined star for our impending Christmas tree, and a package of breadsticks called Kissini, which he had bought for their name. When I got out of bed to make coffee, the sight of the clementines decanted into a clear glass bowl and the honey-colored apple muffins on the dining table was almost as beautiful as that of Lachlan emerging from the bedroom in his T-shirt and Marks & Spencer boxer briefs. I had been thinking my apartment was perfect as it was, but that wasn't the case. I needed something to fill it, and that something was Lachlan.

As much I was over the moon about the place, I was having a hard time finding peace there. I constantly had the urge to fix it—there was always one more thing to buy, or arrange, or clean—making it difficult to read, or watch TV, or kick back in any way. Whenever I tried to take a bath, I would manage for five minutes or so, then I'd feel compelled to leap out to attend to something or other. From the day I arrived with my furniture and boxes of things that I would mostly end up getting rid of to make way for new things, I never felt as relaxed as I did that Sunday.

We lazed around the apartment most of the day, then took a walk to Green-Wood Cemetery, a Brooklyn landmark in whose Gothic gates lived a family of parrots. I wanted to show them to Lach-

Ian because he had a thing for parrots—something to do with his years as a language instructor.

I bought a bird for us to have for dinner, thinking the chilly day called for a stew of chicken and wine, which I call coq au vin, though my own version strays a bit from the traditional French recipe. While the chicken cooked in wine, I soaked in the tub, melting in the warm water and suds.

~~~ ~~~ ~~~ ~~~

Calming Coq au Vin

2 tablespoons olive oil

4 slices pancetta, chopped

1 medium onion, chopped

1 chicken, cut into small pieces

1/2 bottle dry white wine

1 tablespoon butter

6 ounces mushrooms, sliced

1/2 package (5 ounces) frozen peas

1 cup rice

1/4 cup chopped parsley

Warm 1 tablespoon olive oil in a large skillet over high heat; when the oil is hot, add the chicken pieces and brown on all sides.

Meanwhile, in a large Dutch oven warm the other tablespoon of olive oil and add the pancetta; when it is halfway to crisp, add the onion and cook until soft, about 10 minutes. When the pancetta is fully crisp, the onion is soft, and the chicken is browned, add the chicken parts to the Dutch oven and pour in the wine. Remove the fat from the chicken-browning skillet, add the butter and mushrooms, and cook until they give off their water; then add them to the chicken, cover, and cook for 45 minutes. When that time has passed, add the frozen peas and cook an additional 15 minutes.

Fill a large pot with water and bring to a boil, then add rice. Check for doneness after 10 minutes (it may take 15). Drain in a medium strainer and serve chicken over rice on plates. Garnish with chopped parsley.

Serves 2, with leftovers.

I was apprehensive about a few things—like Lachlan's return ticket. The date on it—a few days shy of the absolute limit for visitors without visas to allow for weather conditions that might require Lachlan to fiddle with the date—stayed in my head like a bad song. I was also concerned about keeping up my regular activities while he was staying with me, mostly because I didn't want to miss a moment or meal with my beloved. I would have to find a way to get in the "Core Fusion" (a compilation of yoga, Pilates, and ballet that is offered only at a fancy spa inconveniently located in Manhattan) classes I was taking four times a week and that had become a necessity for my physical and mental health, especially since I had every intention of feeding us well. Then there was my spiritual health, nurtured by Sunday Mass. I had not yet told Lachlan that I was a practicing Catholic, though I had hinted about believing in God. Lachlan didn't chafe at any of my lifestyle requirements; in fact, my fear of being away from him for those hours was for naught. He ended up accompanying me to almost every activity except work (and he showed up there from time to time, too).

Lachlan and I easily fell back into all the routines we had established in August. On Saturday mornings, he would listen to Scottish Premier League football on Radio Scotland, which we got by way of the Internet. He was a fan of Hibernian and would curse out all the other teams that kept his beloved "Hibs" from first-place status. I'd go to the farmer's market and do laundry while he oched and ayed and made all sorts of Gaelic noises to vent his emotions during the game. Then we'd sit down to a British (not English!) breakfast of eggs, bacon, toast, and Heinz baked beans (I wasn't so into the beans). While eating, we listened to *Your Call,* a show for obsessive Scottish football fans who would phone in and wail about the rich Lithuanians who were buying up the local teams, trading players, and causing mayhem. One of the hosts was a woman, and we joked that I should call her to get some sisterly advice about the Hibernian fanatic in my house. We were sure they never got a call from a place as remote as Brooklyn.

Breakfast was the best part of the day. I loved watching Lachlan douse his toast with butter and orange marmalade. He would ask me if I wanted a second piece while he was making his third. I'd always say no, then reluctantly give in, and Lachlan never tired of being amused at the predictable outcome of my indecision. On weekdays, I loathed tearing myself away from him while he sat on the sofa listening to the BBC World Service on the radio. During the day, we'd e-mail each other and talk on the phone, then I'd return in the evening to find him right where I'd left him, reading and wearing two pairs of glasses, his regular distance glasses with reading glasses over them. In between he might have ventured out to the local bookstore; he'd most certainly have made himself lunch and followed that up with a long nap. He seldom left the house unless he was going somewhere with me.

We went to see our long-anticipated Borat movie at a local theater in Park Slope. We got there early, assuming the theater would be packed with our fellow Ali G lovers. Alas, Park Slopers are a little more Charlie Rose than Ali G-there was no one in the theater but us and another woman who happened to be from London. We ended up talking to her because we were sitting there alone with her for such a long time and Lachlan had a hard time biting back on his chattiness. "I pictured seeing this in a big American theater," he said to me right before the lights went down. I spent the entire movie fretting over the fact that I had failed in selecting the correct venue for this most important outing. Why didn't I opt for a gigantic multiplex in Times Square? That was the coming-to-America experience Lachlan was looking for, and here we were sitting with Polly from Pimlico. It was just then that I felt my serenity beginning to take its leave.

Lachlan's problems were of the physical variety. Once he adjusted to the time difference, he came down with a terrible cold; when that went away, he discovered a tiny pimple on the back of his neck that had to be cancer. In the midst of all these woes, Lachlan wasn't "feeling very sexual." Thanksgiving fell in the cold portion of this cycle. I picked up some echinacea on my way home from work on Wednesday and made this lasagna with the leftover mozzarella from the September tasting that I had been saving in the freezer. That's what my mother always made the night before Thanksgiving, a little nod to our other culture, but not the big nod other Italian-American families make of serving pasta as a first course on the holiday. That is a custom my mother finds unconscionable. Don't ask me why—my mother is my mother, is the best reason I can give.

～～～ ～～ ～～

Thanksgiving Eve Lasagna

For meat sauce:

(You can use this sauce with spaghetti or tortellini or any pasta you like.)

1 pound ground beef
2 tablespoons olive oil
1 small yellow onion, chopped
1 clove garlic
Pinch hot red pepper flakes
1 (28-ounce) can tomatoes
1/2 cup red wine
1 teaspoon sugar
1 teaspoon salt
1 cup basil leaves

Brown meat over medium heat until red color is all gone and it is an unattractive gray. Heat olive oil in large skillet over medium heat and add onion, garlic, and red pepper; sauté until garlic is golden and onion is translucent. When meat is fully browned, discard the fat and add meat to the pan with the garlic and onion. Add tomatoes, wine, sugar, and salt; bring to a simmer, lower heat, and cook, stirring occasionally, for 30 minutes. Add basil leaves.

For filling:

2 pounds ricotta

2 eggs, lightly beaten

1/2 teaspoon salt

1/2 cup water

Olive oil for brushing

Here's where I save you a big labor-intensive step:

1 (9-ounce) box no-boil lasagna noodles (I know I disparaged the brand earlier, but Barilla's are good)

4 cups shredded mozzarella (I recommend you shred it yourself with a box grater or food processor fitted with a shredding blade)

1 cup freshly grated parmigiano (I recommend you grate it yourself)

Freshly ground pepper

Preheat oven to 375 degrees.

Mix the ricotta with the eggs, then add salt and water. Brush a 9 by 13-inch baking dish with a little olive oil and a layer of sauce; then arrange the noodles, followed by ricotta, topped with 1 cup of mozzarella, 1/4 cup of parmigiano, and freshly ground pepper, followed by a ladle or two of sauce. Continue this for three layers of filling, then top with one more layer of noodles covered with sauce and sprinkled with the remaining cheese.

Bake for 45 to 50 minutes, until browned and bubbling. Let stand 10 minutes or so before serving.

Serves 8 to 10.

The herbs and cheese got Lachlan well enough to make it to my brother's in Connecticut. I prepared him for insanity, as I do anytime someone I want to impress is about to be confronted with my family, though no one ever thinks they're strange at all. Lachlan found only kindred spirits. "She reminds me of you," he said of Carla, "she sparkles." He discussed Raymond Carver with Matthew and Monty Python with Nick. Nancy, in California, was present by way of Matthew's laptop, which he set on the table to include her in the fun via Skype. This, to Lachlan, was madness, and the rest of us just found it irritating, so I put the computer to sleep while Matthew was too busy cooking and serving to notice.

When I called my mother the next day to ask what she thought of Lachlan, she was enthusiastic. "He's a person you feel instantly comfortable with," she said. It was true. The discomfort, I was about to learn, comes later.

Anne met Lachlan over leftover lasagna the following Saturday, and the two hit it off instantly. Ginia, who had met him over the summer, reconnected with him at a dinner party our friend Meredith gave in honor of his return, but she made herself a little harder to win, not that Lachlan noticed. I showed him off at parties thrown by my *Harper's* colleagues and even dragged him to lunch with the priests. I was hoping that soon Father Joel, whom Lachlan called a "wee soul," could pull off some kind of interfaith ceremony. Apparently, a nod from the bishop was all that was needed to have me married to a Presbyterian.

All the while, we were waiting to hear back from THE AGENT. I had checked in with her a week after Lachlan arrived, the time she'd said it would take her to read the manuscript. She got on the phone with me immediately, bubbling over with praise for the novel: "I just started reading it and I'm pretty positive I'm going to love it, but I haven't finished," she told me. "Don't show it to anyone else, I'll finish in a week." Lachlan made me go over that conversation with him again and again. "Now tell me one more time," he'd say as that week became many more. "Did she say she would call you in a week or that she would finish reading in a week?" I'd make another go at re-creating the conversation as best I could and even refer to the notes I'd made in anticipation of just this sort of hounding.

"What would you want to do if you weren't working in publishing?" Lachlan asked me over dinner at Il Gattopardo in Midtown before a classical music concert at Carnegie Hall (he was an authority on analog music, too). I told him my secret, that I dreamed of being a writer, something I was embarrassed to say, especially since I hadn't written a word since college. Still, that was what I always felt I should be doing, though I was afraid of trying. Lachlan dismissed my aspiration with typical writerly snobbery: "Why would anyone want to be a writer?" he snorted, as if the vocation were a sentence he alone was stuck with for the crime of his brilliance.

Lachlan kept in touch with his parents, calling them every so often to report on the progress of the book. I suppose he liked letting them know that things were happening with his career, and also that he had some kind of girlfriend, because while they were chatting, he asked me by way of hand gestures if I wanted to have a word with his mother. It was the oddest request, but, deciding it connoted commitment I by no means wanted to discourage, I took the phone and spoke with Harriet in Edinburgh, who seemed as uncomfortable as I.

"I see you've discovered the way to Lachlan's heart," she said, having listened to him brag about my cooking for the part of the conversation when he wasn't talking about THE AGENT (from whom we still had no news). How I wished it were so simple. I had gotten to Lachlan's stomach for sure, but I still did not know the anatomical path to his heart, if there even was one.

The route to other parts of his body was difficult to ascertain as well. When the ersatz cancer fear had dissipated, Lachlan had run out of excuses for avoiding sex, so he dug around for some of my ailments. "What do you worry about?" he asked when we got into bed one night. At the time, I was mostly perturbed about the dishwasher—it wasn't draining properly. Lachlan had dealt with the repairman that afternoon while I was at work, but when I opened it that evening, I was confronted with a pool of white stinky water and unclean dishes.

"Everything," I replied to his question, acknowledging that my need to have a home in precise working order is a neurotic balm for a plethora of shortfalls I perceive in my own self.

"I don't know why you worry, you're so intelligent, you're such a wonderful person," Lachlan said—a response that was both truth and overstatement. He construed some of my appliance angst to be about him, which wasn't fair because I didn't know as much as he did about what was going on at that point. If he was right, that little machine had a lot of weight on its racks; there was no service I could call to come and fix Lachlan.

It wasn't all "sand dunes and salty air" the next night when Lachlan embarked on something beyond the usual cuddling in bed, but for all intents and purposes, he appeared to be in the game. Suddenly he stopped. "I'm not excited," he said, "you're anxious, and it's not sexy."

Not the most encouraging pillow talk. "Let's not blow this out of proportion," Lachlan said as I did just that. What is the correct proportion of anguish one should exhibit after being told she is not sexy by the man she loves? Apparently Lachlan knew the ratio.

"I like you full stop," he said as I begged him the next morning to explain to me what was wrong. "All relationships have periods when they're not sexual." Yes, they do, but first shouldn't they go through the one where they are?

Holding hands and cuddling at night continued for a time, but our sex life was officially over. We did, however, continue to sleep together in my bed. Lachlan was apologetic about his frigidity at first; he would embrace me in the kitchen while I was making us dinner and say, "Sorry I'm so weird." He brought me lilies, which "symbolize virginity"—an inappropriate message, though they were pretty and filled the apartment with a glorious scent—he brought me a nice bottle of Nebbiolo, one of my favorite grapes. But louder than the fragrances and fine tastes were the words *you're not sexy.* My senses were overloaded with the sound of that phrase.

The burning question in my mind, whether the problem was with him or me, should have easily been answered by the fact that Lachlan was developing an unnatural affection for an ice-cream scoop—a purple plastic object shaped like a little man with a round head that scoops ice cream and a pear-shaped body for a handle. Lachlan christened him "Scoopy" and insisted he be liberated from his drawer and stand on his cloven foot on the kitchen countertop. One Friday evening, Lachlan brought him out to the living room to watch *Chitty Chitty Bang Bang* with us and for the next few days changed the lyrics to one of the songs from the movie in homage: "Someone to care for, to be there for; we have Scoopy," he'd sing. He referred to Scoopy constantly as our child, the third person in our home. He even did this in front of my mother!

"Scoopy was very upset!" Lachlan exclaimed to me in private after she'd laughed off his peculiarity. I was enchanted by the Scoopy thing and even sang along to his anthems, though life with Lachlan was becoming wretched.

The other thing Lachlan loved that was not me was coffee. Not that it kept him awake, but he adored drinking it, and he was an authority on making it. He devoted himself to the study of techniques for maximizing the beverage's flavor potential and had many well-researched ideas on the matter. I learned from Lachlan that you should never clean a coffeemaker (or teapot, while we're at it) with soap—it should be rinsed simply with water and only water. A new espresso maker must be seasoned before use; to do this, you brew a mock pot of coffee from used grinds. (I suppose if you're not thrifty, you could brew a pot from new grinds and throw out the first batch. But then, why not just drink it and grin and bear a first, imperfect cup of coffee?) Lachlan insisted on the fine grind, no matter the filter, the better to wrench every last bit of flavor out of the bean. He treated coffee with an Old Testament sort of reverence; it was veneration mingled with fear. He saw dangers inherent in adding fire to ground beans and water under pressure. To make a cup of espresso was to flirt with death. If the pot was left boiling on the stove one moment longer than necessary, it might explode and shoot boiling water and grinds all over the kitchen. We could be killed! Lachlan kept constant vigil over espresso as it brewed, making sure to remove the pot from the heat at just the right moment, to keep us safe.

I don't follow any of his dictums. Do you actually think I would take coffee-making advice from someone who sleeps all the time?

As I got more and more fed up, my generosity waned. I begrudged Lachlan the littlest things—like the pricey can of Italian tuna fish he helped himself to for lunch every day. That was a habit I could break, knowing full well how Lachlan obsessed about his health. Apparently, he was not aware of the dangerously high mercury content in tuna fish. I felt it was my duty to let him know that it wasn't a good idea to eat it every day. Instantly, he was on to more economical lunch options, like beans and toast.

Lachlan's lack of concern for the needs of my body, a body that was shouldering the burden of procuring for him a big-deal New York agent, was doing me in. One rainy Monday morning when I was going to have to phone her for the fifth time, I woke up crying and I couldn't stop. I tried to explain to Lachlan how the pressure was getting to me; how much energy it took to make those calls. He sent me off with good wishes and a pursed-lipped kiss, as he did every day.

My discontent reverberated onto my entertaining, usually so free of incident. During the Scottish occupation, a fire broke out at two separate dinner parties. The first time Jen and Jeff were over for my mother's trusty baked sole, a fish that proved trickier than it needed to be because when I pulled the baking sheets from the oven to see how they were doing, they slid to the back, spilling grease onto the oven floor and causing flames to shoot out wildly. Lachlan was in the living room yukking it up with the guests while my eyelashes and hair were getting singed in the kitchen. Jeff finally heard my cries and ran in to put out the fire. It was then I realized that the previous owner of my apartment had inserted the racks backward. That discovery put an end to some of the near death experiences, but not all of them.

~~~ ~~~ ~~~ ~~~

Incendiary Sole

   1/4 cup (1/2 stick) butter, melted
   1/3 cup olive oil
   1 heaping cup bread crumbs
   3/4 teaspoon salt
   1 tablespoon chopped parsley
   Freshly ground pepper
   2 pounds sole or flounder

Preheat oven to 375 degrees.

Combine butter and oil in a wide, shallow bowl; season the bread crumbs with salt, parsley, and pepper and spread on a plate. Dip the fish in the butter and oil, covering thoroughly, then dredge through the bread crumbs. Place on a baking sheet and bake for about 15 minutes, until the crumb topping is lightly browned. (Don't worry, I've adjusted the recipe so there is no extraneous fat that might cause an oven fire.)

Serves 4 to 6.

I took off the Friday before Christmas to get a tree with Lachlan. I had never had my own Christmas tree before because my previous living room would not accommodate one. Unfortunately, the heartwarming scene of dragging a fresh Vermont fir through the Brooklyn streets that danced in my head when I had envisioned Christmas with Lachlan a month earlier did not play according to script. Besides the fact that it was raining, yet again, dragging such an exultant symbol down sidewalks with a man whom you want to love you more than anything else in the world, who doesn't and won't no matter how many pretty decorations you come up with, filled me with gloom.

It rained on Christmas Day, too. For my present, Lachlan gave me a cutting board designed for slicing bread with slats for the crumbs to drop through, making an altogether neater bread-cutting experience. A gift as sexy as our relationship, you might say, but that's what I asked for when he asked me what I wanted. I was shocked that he was planning on getting me anything, but Lachlan believed in presents. I got him a beautifully designed edition of the chapter on greatness from Baldassare Castiglione's *Book of the Courtier,* a book I loved back in my innocent college days, which my current situation recalled to me.

The week between Christmas and New Year's Day, I gave a dinner party for out-of-town friends who were in New York for the holiday. They had been hearing about Lachlan by e-mail and were looking forward to meeting him. Too bad that by that time our relationship was as deflated as cooled Yorkshire pudding. Which is what I happened to be making that evening, along with roast beef, for the traditional British Sunday dinner (even though it was Wednesday). My puddings looked and tasted perfect when I pulled them from the oven after extinguishing a fire caused by the fat that bubbled over in the pan. This time, Lachlan got wind of the crisis and ran in with a broom (?)

to put it out. The handle hit the overhead light, causing glass to shatter all over the floor, so once we had the flames under control we were sweeping up this other mess. Besides that, the meat was tough. I didn't have a good time at that dinner, but that was par for the course, and this was no St. Andrews Links.

~~ ~~ ~~ ~~

Spiced Roast Beef

(Adapted from epicurious.com)

Your meat won't be tough unless you have a withholding Scotsman living in your house.

- 1 teaspoon whole cumin
- 1 teaspoon whole coriander
- 1 teaspoon whole black peppercorns
- 1 teaspoon salt
- 1/2 teaspoon ground ginger
- 1/8 teaspoon cayenne
- 1 garlic clove, thinly sliced
- 1 (3-pound) beef eye roast
- 2 tablespoons olive oil
- 2 tablespoons fresh cilantro, chopped

Preheat oven to 350 degrees.

Crush cumin, coriander, and black pepper in a mortar and pestle, process them in a food processor, or put them in a paper or plastic bag and crack them with a rolling pin or hammer. Mix in salt, ginger, and cayenne with crushed spices. With a paring knife, make several small slits all over the meat; inset garlic into them. Brush meat with the oil and rub spice mixture over it.

Roast until a meat thermometer inserted into the center registers 120 degrees for medium-rare; this should take 50 minutes to 1 hour. When it is done, remove the meat to a cutting board, tent it with foil, and let it rest for 10 minutes or so. Slice thinly and sprinkle with cilantro.

Serves 6 to 8.

～～～ ～～ ～～ ～～

Yorkshire Pudding

1 heaping cup flour
1/4 teaspoon salt

1 cup milk
2 eggs, lightly beaten
4 tablespoons butter, melted

In a bowl, stir together flour, salt, and milk until well mixed, then add the eggs and stir until batter is smooth. Let it stand at room temperature for 1 hour.

When ready to bake, preheat oven to 375 degrees. Distribute the melted butter among 8 muffin molds, then evenly distribute the batter into the molds and bake until puffed up and golden brown, about 15 to 20 minutes. Remove from oven and serve immediately. Yorkshire puddings deflate rapidly, like expectations.

Yield: 8 puddings.

It rained on New Year's Eve and then again on New Year's Day, two of the dreariest days of my entire life. Ginia gave a dinner party, and at midnight I did not receive a kiss from my date. I told myself that maybe in Europe people don't kiss their girlfriend, or friend, or career manager, or whatever the heck I was, to ring in the New Year. I went out on the terrace to smoke a cigarette and tore my new skirt while climbing over the windowsill to get out there. I focused my vexation on that for the rest of the night.

The next morning, we awoke to more rain. I could barely drag myself out of bed, let alone to the party I planned to attend (hosted by more friends who couldn't wait to meet Lachlan). Ginia was supposed to go, but she backed out. Anne was wavering. I didn't want to go to the party, but I sure didn't want to spend the day at home alone with Lachlan. I was paralyzed under the covers with my phone, trying to cajole someone into coming along.

Anne reluctantly agreed to join us, and while Lachlan was consumed with charming some obese lady, she and I stuffed our faces with Rice Krispies treats painted green and shaped like wreaths. That's when I finally came clean to her about what was going on at my house. When you're stuck in a situation like the one I was in, you don't want to tell your friends because that means admitting to yourself that it's really happening—but once you do, it becomes so much more bearable. The melted marshmallow and unburdening made me feel a little less alone. On the way home, now that I was thinking myself slightly less doomed, Lachlan, Anne, and I talked about resolutions for the coming year. You know what Lachlan's was. Anne and I talked about writing our own books, something we had been talking about for a few months, though neither of us had any idea what we would write about; we just had the nagging sense that we should be writing something. "You're such an amazing cook, you should write a cookery book," Lachlan said. That idea wasn't "daft," as Lachlan might say, if only I could come up with a cookery book idea. I had no clue how one would come to me, but on that dark day, I felt a glimmer of hope that I could. Then I forgot about it for a while.

While I drowned in rain and agony, Lachlan and I continued doing everything together. We visited museums, ate dinner, went to the movies. Watching *The Last King of Scotland* was like seeing a twist on my own predicament; I felt as if I were being hung by my skin, only not by Idi Amin, but by the cute Scotsman. At the Guggenheim on a Friday evening (when it's free), Lachlan kept his arm around me as we ascended and descended the curving ramp. He bought me a postcard of a painting I liked of monks eating dinner and propped it up on my bedside in front of one of an Annunciation he had bought me in happier times at the Philadelphia Museum of Art.

Lachlan used a variety of terms to refer to himself in regard to me. Sometimes he was my "boyfriend," sometimes he was my "friend." When he became "the guy living in your apartment," I had to make inquiries.

"Could you please explain our relationship?" I asked one Saturday morning after the Hibs game.

We sat on the settee in the foyer, where he put his arms around me and said, "We have a very warm friendship."

I pushed him away. What did I need with a warm friendship? I had more friends than I knew what to do with, and I certainly didn't handle their careers.

I cried every day after that conversation. We talked about him finding someplace else to live for his last few weeks, but I couldn't bear the thought of him leaving. Either way I was going to be miserable, so why inconvenience Lachlan, too? It was Stockholm syndrome all over again, no cure on the horizon, no plans for a benefit.

Even though the ecstatic promise of our union was short-lived (for me, at least; there was plenty of promise left in it for him), I continued to think that we had a true connection and that Lachlan had shut himself off from allowing it to blossom. "What is love if not what we have?" I pleaded with him. "We like all

the same things, we're happy eating together, living together, watching TV together." I just couldn't let go of the joy I
felt in our first few days together and the
sentiments enclosed in the hundreds of
notes we batted back and forth across the
ocean. How did he lose all desire for me?
Was I too nervous, as he had suggested?
Should I have let him cook, acted a little
more helpless? But then, how helpless
can the person orchestrating your literary career pretend to be?

"The only thing wrong with you is that
you think something is wrong with you,"
Lachlan said, which is plenty perceptive,
but served only to make me hate myself
more for thinking there was something
wrong with me and wondering if Lachlan would love me if I could stop thinking that.

Lachlan, on the other hand, thought
there was absolutely nothing wrong with
him, an admirable quality indeed. "This
is me, this is the way I am," he declared.
"I've never been able to commit to a

woman, and I'm happy that way." And the itinerant life? He was happy with that, too.

"I'm still me, I'm still Lachlan," he said, not understanding why I didn't want to talk to him. I holed up in my bedroom, reading Patricia Marx, an author Lachlan discovered one day at the local bookstore. Flipping through her novel *Him Her Him Again the End of Him,* he thought he had found his literary soul mate. I got jealous when he told me this and immediately procured a copy for myself (know thy rivals). This funny novel about an intelligent woman who over many years will not be dissuaded of her love for a heinous cad served as a good escape in those days. Lachlan, on the other hand, found his interest waning as he read further. It was comforting to learn that I wasn't the only woman he quickly lost excitement for.

As I took to hiding in my bedroom and going out to dinner without him, Lachlan began to play the injured. "I feel like I've lost a friend," he said when I came home from an evening out with Anne. "I've waited for you for ice cream, have you had dessert?" I loosened up a little eating Häagen-Dazs banana split and watching the Fleetwood Mac *Behind the Music* on VH-1. Then Christine McVie singing "Songbird" had me weeping all over again.

Perhaps it was my hysteria that emboldened Lachlan to venture out of the house one afternoon without alerting me or showing up at my office as he always did, even now that things were just awful, which he always pretended wasn't the case. I was calling the house to tell him something or other, but there was no answer. I never thought for a moment that he had walked out— he wouldn't do that anyway, he had nowhere to go. I jumped to the only possible conclusion: He was dead—his bile tube detonated or that faulty electric charge in his heart had claimed him once and for all. He was asleep when I left for work—at this point in our relationship, I was happy when he missed breakfast, giving me the chance to sneak a cigarette and blow smoke out the living room window—I didn't think to check if he was still breathing.

When I finally heard from him, just when I was about to go home to collect his remains, I was livid. "Just make us something for dinner!" I barked (odd that that's what I would come up with as a punishment).

When I came home, he served me this delicious farfalle with zucchini and eggs. "It's a natural combination," he told me. I sure hadn't thought of it, but it is indeed delectable. The eggs give the dish a wonderful creaminess. It is another Lachlan creation that I continue to re-create.

Lachlan's Farfalle with Zucchini and Egg

2 tablespoons olive oil

1/2 medium onion, chopped

2 medium zucchini squash (1 green, 1 yellow)
1 teaspoon salt
1/2 pound farfalle
2 eggs
2 heaping tablespoons freshly grated
   parmigiano, plus extra for passing at table
Freshly ground pepper
1/4 cup chopped parsley

In a medium sauté pan, warm olive oil over medium heat, then add the chopped onion and cook until opaque, 3 to 4 minutes. Slice zucchini into 1/2-inch rounds, then each round into quarters; add zucchini and salt to the onions and cook until soft, 15 to 20 minutes.

Meanwhile, cook the farfalle according to the directions for pasta on page 32. Beat the eggs and add parmigiano; set aside. When pasta is cooked, drain and add to zucchini mixture. Remove from heat, add the eggs, and allow them to cook on the hot pasta. Serve in warmed bowls garnished with fresh-

ly ground pepper and chopped parsley.
Pass extra cheese at table.

Serves 2, with leftovers.

A few weeks before Lachlan's departure, THE AGENT finally let me know that she was going to take on his book. It was all bittersweet to me, though I feigned great excitement, and in some ways I was excited that I had succeeded brilliantly at my fool's errand. I handed Lachlan a situation any writer would kill for, and I was the one being killed for it. I made him take me out for a "celebratory" dinner at a local Italian restaurant I had been raving to him about, a newfangled mom-and-pop place like the one we'd talked about opening in sunnier days. Lachlan wasn't impressed with his tortelloni or his tagliata. "Your food is so much better," he said. Of course it is—mine's free.

THE AGENT arranged a round of meetings for Lachlan with a handful of interested publishers. She guessed that she could get $50,000 for the book, a number Lachlan and I had been imagining all along. I intended to see the book through and to see him onto his plane—after all, I had a lot of my own blood, sweat, and tears invested in the project. Yes, I even considered driving him to the airport, going so far as to make arrangements with my mother to borrow her car. "Do you think it looks funny?" asked my mother, who now was sickened by the sight of Lachlan, when I told her I wouldn't need to use it after all. I think her question explains a lot about why I am as nuts as I am.

The night before Lachlan left, I was full of righteous anger. I walked to Dean & DeLuca to pick up food for his last meal, muttering to myself about how sick and tired of him I was and how happy that I wasn't going to have to make his damn dinner anymore, all the while wondering what I would make. I decided on the teriyaki pork I had gotten there before. They sell it already marinated so you just have to put it in the oven. I wasn't hungry when I got home; I sat on the couch and just stared at the opposite wall, where there happened to be a mirror, in which I watched Lachlan put his arm around me.

"What are you feeling?" he asked.

"Nothing," I said, "I'm just sick of you."

When he asked me to get his rucksack out of my storage bin in the basement, I was more than delighted to do it.

~~~ ~~~ ~~~

Lachlan's Last Supper

Teriyaki Pork Loin

> 1/2 cup teriyaki sauce
> 1 clove garlic, minced
> 1 tablespoon minced ginger
> 2 scallions sliced, green parts only
> 1 pound pork tenderloin

Combine all ingredients in a Ziploc bag. Marinate on the kitchen counter for 30 minutes or up to 8 hours in the refrigerator.

Roast in a 425-degree oven until pork is cooked to your liking, 20 to 25 minutes. It's a trying time, but this pork is tender!

Yield: 2 servings.

~~~ ~~~ ~~~ ~~~

Cilantro Rice

(Adapted from *Gourmet* magazine)

3/4 cup rice
1 1/2 tablespoons olive oil
1 clove garlic, minced
1 cup chopped cilantro
1 1/2 cups water
2 tablespoons pine nuts, toasted
Salt, to taste

Cook rice as you would pasta, in lightly salted boiling water. Check for softness after 10 minutes; it could take up to 15. Drain and toss gently with oil, garlic, cilantro, and pine nuts. Taste for salt.

Serves 2.

Bok Choy with Garlic

(Adapted from *Bon Appétit* magazine)

1 clove garlic, minced
1 tablespoon olive oil
4 baby bok choy
3/4 cup chicken broth
Salt and pepper to taste

In a medium skillet over medium heat, sauté garlic and olive oil for 1 minute. Add bok choy and broth, bring to a simmer, and cook for 8 to 10 minutes, turning occasionally. Season with salt and pepper to taste.

Serves 2.

Three publishers were set to make offers on Lachlan's book the day of his flight back to Italy, where he would freeload some more until he figured out his next step. THE AGENT instructed everyone to have bids in by noon. That morning, I had to go to the funeral of my uncle. We weren't very close, so it wasn't a devastating event; still, it added some more emotion to the biblical flood I was already feeling. Lachlan was packing when I returned.

"Well?" I asked.

"Random House offered a hundred and ten thousand dollars," he said.

Now added to the loss of a love, and a relative, was a sense of having been swindled of everything I ever owned. I sat on the floor at the threshold to my bedroom, where Lachlan was fussing with his clothes and books, and smoked cigarette after cigarette while I tried to find out once and for all why he didn't love me. Goddamn it! If I could get him $110,000 for a book about a rhinoceros, he was going to give me an answer!

"That's grown-up money, are you going to grow up now?"

"Maybe I'll use it to go on living like a child," he said petulantly.

"I did that so that you and I could have a life together."

"I don't love you," he said.

At those words I moved to the bed, where I flopped around like a just caught fish. "There's no one in the world I would have done that for. I wouldn't have done it for myself!"

"You didn't do everything," he said, "it's not like I didn't spend ten years writing the book."

A person who could stay in one place could have easily written that book in a year—was all I could think.

"Who would you love? What were the people you loved like? Did you love Sasha [the Australian artist]?"

"I think I did." (That was a reinterpretation of history as originally told to me.)

"Why?"

"Because she had a pet kangaroo," Lachlan joked, "because she had an Australian accent."

"Did you *ever* love me?"

"I was excited about you," he replied.

Which sounded like nothing other than: "I was excited about what you could do for me."

Lachlan wanted to take me out to lunch, but I had no appetite (he couldn't believe it), so he went about reheating the previous night's dinner. I sat with him and I ate and that did make me feel a wee bit better. We sat on the couch together the last few moments.

"You never even apologized," I said.

"You haven't given me any space to."

It was time for him to leave. I was sobbing hysterically. There were tears in Lachlan's eyes, too, as we hugged and he walked out my door for the last time.

I called my mother, still crying hysterically. She cried, too.

Then I called Anne, who was warm and sensible.

Then I called Ginia, who was on a deadline, but I saw her later.

Then I smoked six more cigarettes.

Then I took a nap.

The next day, I started writing my book.

"What do you want to know?" it opened. "How much money he got for the book or how much he broke my heart?" I imagined an entire book about Lachlan, ending with the line "Reader, they overpaid."

But then I thought, Why let him alone have all the glory? even though that experience, the first to leave me feeling both heartbroken *and* used, certainly was the grated cheese atop the bowl of spaghetti. I wrote about all of them, and I kept on cooking.

I was preparing a Sunday afternoon dinner for Larisa and her family. While cutting potatoes with my new Wüsthof chef's knife (I was buying a lot of things for my apartment after Lachlan left, trying to make it look a little less like the place where he lived—I did keep Scoopy, but he has to stay in his drawer unless he's working), I cut a gash through my thumb and ended up spending five hours in the emergency room getting seven stitches. I reluctantly canceled my dinner party (I actually thought I might be able to get sewn up and home in time to finish cooking), and my frantic mother came over to cook the food that I left strewn about my kitchen. Before she arrived I sent Nick, who had taken me to the hospital, back to my place to wipe the blood off the walls. Matthew stayed with me while I was getting sewn up.

As I was lying there waiting to be mended, I thought about how much I had suffered for the love of cooking and love itself, those two interchangeable passions. My body was marked by wounds that represented both of them—my arms were scarred from burns, my thumb was severed, my heart was broken. There had to be something for food to give me. And there was.

I went back to the book. I never doubted it would turn out okay.

I look forward to the day I can say that about love . . . but that's the next book.

Baci e abbracci a . . .

Ginia Bellafante, who dreams for me even when I'm not dreaming for myself. Her friendship and influence over these many years has enriched my life in countless ways.

Jennifer Warren, who has been listening to me and encouraging me ever since our fairly innocent college days; her generosity of heart is infinite.

Anne Magruder, who was a font of warmth, daily inspiration, and laughter throughout the writing of this book and for many years beforehand.

Frank Bruni, who explained my idea better than I could and brought it to . . .

Lisa Bankoff, who shared my joy in this

project, handled it with the utmost care, and is, best of all, a terrific girlfriend.

Caryn Karmatz Rudy, whose enthusiasm for this book has been unwavering and who lent understanding and deep intelligence to its every page.

Jennifer Romanello, a friend I met through work who became like family and was there through many of these stories, laughing at them when they were funny and helping me to shake them off when they no longer were. How fortunate that this book ended up in her sage hands!

Sandy Sislowitz, who changed my life dramatically with phenomenal insight, deep compassion, and abundant humor.

Corey Seymour for being a teacher, a guide, a source of sustenance, amusement, and wisdom for far longer than I deserve.

Lucinda Rosenfeld and John Cassidy for reminding me—over many evenings of spaghetti and meatballs traded for their excellent company—that I am a pretty good cook.

Meredith Tucker for being a fantastic neighbor, cheerleader, and taster.

Russell Perreault and Reed Maroc for impeccable hospitality and countless incredible meals at their beautiful home in the Connecticut hills.

Colleagues at *Harper's Magazine,* especially Ellen Rosenbush, Jennifer Szalai, and Ted Ross—who kindly read the proposal in its early stages and offered editorial guidance. I was privileged to be in the company of so many smart people for so many years and I am privileged to get to keep them for friends.

Mark Lane, Dennis Corrado, Joel Warden, Anthony Andreassi, and James Simon at The Brooklyn Oratory for being so keen on a book I'll have to go to confession for.

Anne Twomey for designing a book jacket that captured exactly what I wanted when I had no idea what I wanted.

Jamie Raab, Emi Battaglia, Martha Otis, Karen Torres, Elly Weisenberg, Amanda Englander, Harvey-Jane Kowal, Sona Vogel, Brad Negbaur, and everyone at Grand Central Publishing.

Karolina Sutton, Tina Wexler, and Elizabeth Perrella at ICM.

Kenneth Ardito, Maxwell Ardito, Susanna Beacom, Gillian Blake, Bliss Broyard, Carmen D'Aloia, Larisa DePalma, Jeff Edelson, Jonathan Elderfield, Marianne Gillow, Mark Haag, Yuki Hirayama, Hannah Houston, Deborah Kwan, Dante Nicola Melucci, Elizabeth Melucci, Stella Giulia Melucci, Biba Milioto, Deak Nabers, Blake Nelson, Alessandro Pugliese, Giulia Rosina Pugliese, Stanislao Pugliese, Maria Ricapito, Joia Speciale, Robert Sullivan, Suzanne Sullivan, Jen Tadaki Catanzariti, Marie Ventura, Elena von Kassel, Angela Voulangas, and Jimmy Wallenstein.

And, as if so many incredible friends weren't enough, I have been blessed with two sisters and two brothers whose love for me and pride in me have always been palpable and unshakable: a lifetime of thanks to Nancy, Carla, Nicholas, and Matthew.

Recipe Index